To: _____

───∽❧∽───

"For it is God who works in you
to will and to act
according to his good purpose"
(Phil. 2:13).

───∽❧∽───

From: _____

Unleashing Your Potential

Discovering Your God-Given Opportunities for Ministry

Frank R. Tillapaugh

Regal Books

A Division of GL Publications
Ventura, California, U.S.A.

Published by Regal Books
A Division of GL Publications
Ventura, California 93006
Printed in U.S.A.

Any omission of credits is unintentional. The publisher requests documentation
for future printings.

Library of Congress Cataloging-in-Publication Data applied for.

1 2 3 4 5 6 7 8 9 10/ 92 91 90 89 88

Rights for publishing this book in other languages are contracted by Gospel
Literature International (GLINT) foundation. GLINT also provides technical
help for the adaptation, translation, and publishing of Bible study resources
and books in scores of languages worldwide. For further information, contact
GLINT, Post Office Box 488, Rosemead, California, 91770, U.S.A., or the
publisher.

To Mary, God's special gift
to help me unleash my potential.

Contents

**Part Three:
Unleashing Your Potential**

Acknowledgments

Several people have contributed to both *Unleashing* books. Julia Castle Wright and Barbara Linville spent many hours on the manuscript of the first book. Barbara was also a great help with this book along with Fritz Ridenour and Earl Roe. Lois Stokes put together most of the information found in the "Classified List of Parachurch Organizations." And a special word of thanks to Mary Beckwith who spent many hours helping me work through this material.

Introduction

Since the publication of my first book *Unleashing the Church,* I've been invited to speak throughout the United States, Canada and overseas. On nearly all of these occasions, I've addressed the issue of the local church's inability to do effective ministry.

As I've traveled widely these past few years, it has become clear nearly everyone in the Christian community agrees the "fortress mentality" dominates the vast majority of our churches today. The typical scenario in the fortress church is to buy land, build buildings and concentrate nearly all its ministry efforts within the walls of those buildings.

Fortress thinking is not a problem peculiar to any particular region of the United States nor to the rest of the world. Neither is it characteristic of any particular denomination. Yet fortress mentalities have produced fortress churches and such churches dominate so thoroughly that when we see a church with a handful of internal programs, we accept it as being a "normal church."

The domination of fortress thinking has produced an enormous amount of frustration in our churches. An example of that frustration appeared in *Christianity Today* when the Reformed Theological Seminary in Jackson, Mississippi ran an ad declaring: "Before anyone can become an effective and consistent minister of the gospel, he or she must have a deep desire to do so. As most people ponder what it takes for the average lay person to become an effective minister, the first thing that normally comes to mind is training. That thinking is a big mistake. The first thing needed is desire."

- More than 75 percent of the churches in America are no longer growing, or are experiencing a decline in membership.
- Most people who do not attend church say worship services are boring and irrelevant.
- Ordained clergy are leaving the ministry in unprecedented numbers, and one out of every eight pastors is thinking of resigning.[1]

It's frustrating for seminaries, which exist primarily to train leadership for churches, to be faced with the above information. Frustration also runs high in parachurch organizations trying to assist the local church.

Much of the dilemma we face today stems from the fact that we have very few ministry expectations in the local church. We expect worship services, Sunday Schools and choirs. But no one expects churches to get involved in ministries with alcoholics or abused children.

Fortunately, however, not only is there widespread frustration in our churches today, there is also widespread optimism. There's a growing confidence the second generation following World War II can change the way it thinks about the Church and its ministry.

But that change must begin with the individual believer, who must be able to envision his or her potential for ministry. The average Christian must stop thinking about a special group of people as "the ministers" and start thinking about their own ability to minister to another's needs.

In his letter to the Ephesians, Paul is talking to the entire Church when he says: "For we are God's workmanship, created in Christ Jesus to do good works, which God prepared in advance for us to do" (2:10).

This book is written to every Christian, with the emphasis on developing our personal lives in order to become ministry-oriented people, using God's Word and examples of others who have answered His call.

My prayer is that as you read the pages that follow you will become more ministry-minded. And furthermore that you will be encouraged to pursue your ministry potential within the context of your local church.

I believe we have made a grave mistake in abandoning the local church as we attempt to work out our ministry calling. Unfortunately, however, we have had no other choice. In essence, we have been forced to look outside the local church to unleash our God-given potential for ministry.

If lay members feel called to teach Sunday School, usher or sponsor a youth ministry, they find plenty of opportunity within his or her own church. Others are forced into a spectator role, having to be satisfied with the challenge to have good Christian testimonies and be witnesses in their general life-style. But we can be thankful there is growing optimism that churches can and should become more aggressive and innovative in ministering to the community.

Therefore, we want to address this book to individual believers with the assumption we are entering an era when there will be more freedom to pursue a wide range of ministry opportunities within the local church.

Of course there will be times when Christians will want to minister through organizations other than the local church. But the entire Christian community, local churches and parachurch organizations as well, will be better off when churches are designed where everyone can minister.

Before anyone can become an effective and consistent minister of the gospel, he or she must have a deep desire to do so. As most people ponder what it takes for the average lay person to become an effective minister the first thing that normally comes to mind is training. That thinking is a big mistake. The first thing needed is desire.

From experience I have learned that if people do not have the desire to get involved in ministry, it doesn't matter how well-trained or gifted they are. But where does that desire come from?

The apostle Paul wrote to the believers in Philippi: "For it is God who is at work within you, giving you the will and power to achieve his purpose" (Phil. 2:13, Phillips).

So, the desire for ministry comes from God. Churches can do a great deal to cultivate and encourage that desire, but not create it. That's why the promise of Philippians

2:13 is so encouraging. It assures us that God is working in us giving us the desires He wants us to have. He is not only giving us desires in harmony with His purposes, He has also given us spiritual gifts and the power to achieve those desires.

While training people for ministry is not the most critical factor, it is extremely important. Fortunately we live in a day of unparalleled resources and opportunities to train the average person for ministry. Denominational agencies, schools, parachurch organizations, as well as churches themselves, are producing new ideas and tools for training lay people at an astonishing rate. When it comes to resources for training people to be ministers we are the most blessed generation in the history of the Church. We ought to be encouraged.

I believe we are entering an age of unprecedented impact by lay ministers. Coupling the scriptural promises we have just read with the widespread optimism that the time has come to challenge the fortress mentality that has dominated our churches for so long, we can pursue unleashing our potential with optimism and confidence.

Note
1. *Christianity Today* (Feb. 7, 1986), p. 14.

PART ONE
From the Fortress to the Front Lines

CHAPTER 1

What's Wrong with the Fortress Mentality?

Nowhere does the Bible exhort the world to come to the Church. Rather, as Dick Halverson has reminded us, God's Great Commission makes it clear the Church must go to the world.[1]

Unfortunately, most of our churches today evidence little of ministries that result from members of the Body going out into the world. And the primary reason for that is what we term the "fortress mentality."

In my earlier book *Unleashing the Church*, I discussed at length the concept of fortress mentality and how that kind of mind-set is limiting, sometimes even paralyzing, our efforts to penetrate our communities with the gospel and to do effective ministry.

Instead, many parachurch organizations have sprung up in recent years in an effort to fill the needs of people, needs the Church should really be addressing.

David McKenna, in his book *Mega Truth*, writes:

> In the past World War II years of the 20th century we saw the spectacular rise of what has euphemistically been called "parachurch ministries" such as Youth for Christ, InterVarsity Fellowship, Young Life and Campus Crusade for Christ. Essentially, they webe created in response to the knowledge and the need of the post-war baby boom. Traditional church structures . . . did not process the information or respond to the need with speed and flexibility *required to take the gospel to youth rather than waiting for them to come to the church* [emphasis mine].

McKenna goes on to make a statement some may dispute, but one I think is right on target:

> Yet if the facts were known, parachurch ministries may well have been the catalysts for the "Born Again" movement of the '70s from which evangelical churches benefited by spiritual renewal, numerical growth and public visibility. [2]

No doubt the rise of the paraministries has been in proportion to the domination of the fortress mentality in our churches.

JUST WHAT IS THE FORTRESS MENTALITY?

In a few words, the fortress mentality says the church will minister to anyone who will come within the four walls of

our church buildings, and fit in with us. Sound a bit crude?
Think about it for a moment.

---

*Our culture's biggest need is for the very
gospel message and value system our
churches have to offer. To meet that need,
the local church—the visible manifestation
of the Body of Christ—is ordained to be
His witness, to be salt and light to the
world.*

A typical church in twentieth-century America probably started out in a rather small facility. When it began to
see some growth, members decided they needed a larger
facility, so started a building program, while looking for
property and drawing up plans for a new building.

Once into its new facility, Sunday School classes were
set up, the choir grew into its new loft and maybe a men's
and women's ministry program was started. A sign was
probably erected outside the front door listing the times
for worship services, Sunday School and Bible study, along
with the pastor's name and a note at the bottom saying:
Everyone Welcome.

To its parishioners, the call was to teach Sunday
School, join the choir and fix meals for shut-ins and pot-
lucks. Otherwise, just come and fit in. The overwhelming
majority of churches today are fortress-type churches.

THE FOCUS OF FORTRESS CHURCHES

Now let's take a quick look at the ministry focus of many, if
not all, of these fortress-type churches. It's clear the vast

majority of programs and ministries in these churches are built exclusively around the middle-class family. Ministries that do not fit neatly into the middle-class scheme of things have simply been ignored.

For example, a great need in our communities is for ministries to street people. This need is becoming greater, with the number of homeless persons growing every day. Yet, how many of today's typical churches have street people coming to worship? Another great need today is for young unwed mothers to be loved and shepherded. How many young unwed mothers feel comfortable and loved enough to be sitting in our pews on Sunday mornings? Nevertheless, street people and unwed mothers, as well as many others outside the walls of our churches, need the love, concern and message of the gospel that we inside the walls of fortress churches have to offer.

In addition to ignoring these cultural "lower level" groups, local churches appear to be blind to the enormous opportunity we have to evangelize tomorrow's world leaders who are studying in the United States. Internationals, in contrast to street people, are a type of "upper level" target group. Amazingly, we spend millions to send missionaries overseas, yet we've made so little effort to minister to foreigners in our own country.

What can explain such a glaring oversight in our response to the Great Commission? Simply that internationals are not part of white middle-class America, and, again, anyone outside of middle-class family units has been, on the whole, ignored by our churches.

We are not advocating that we stop doing the typical ministries of the fortress church. We need to continue to develop the middle-class ministries God has blessed over the years. But we also must develop a whole new range of ministries as well.

We need to unleash the masses of people who are currently inside the walls of the fortress churches, those who have been saved and nurtured through the ministries that have taken place inside the walls, to reach out to a hurting and dying world.

Think of the manpower potential in our churches today—literally millions of persons. Those millions, by the way, are a testimony to the effectiveness not only of the paraministries, but of the fortress ministries as well. Certainly a lot of great ministry has gone on through traditional inside-the-walls programs. But, can you imagine the impact of unleashing those millions? If that happens we will truly confront this generation with the good news of Jesus Christ, as we fill needs and see changed lives all around us.

THE SUCCESS OF PARACHURCH MINISTRIES

Over the years, large numbers of parachurch organizations have sprung up in our communities, reaching out to hurting people with love, comfort, support, health care and many other expressions of concern that the rest of us take for granted. And these organizations are often quite successful at what they do.

Why?

First of all, most parachurch organizations are not limited to meeting in a certain place. Nor do they confine their ministries within the walls of a particular church building. Rather, they go where the people and their needs are, giving these organizations a tremendous flexibility lacking in local churches.

Second, such organizations tend to be more effective

in stimulating the vision and commitment of lay volunteers. Local churches often stimulate the lay person's vision with the challenge to imagine the building of a facility or the kinds of events that can take place inside such a facility. Churches do little to capitalize on the burden, the call and vision a lay person might have for a certain group or type of people beyond the walls of the church building.

The ministries that take place in the church are just not enough, if we are to fulfill the Great Commission. We must take our ministries from the fortress to the front lines.

Parachurch organizations, on the other hand, solicit, cultivate, train and utilize such people.

All of this raises two crucial questions:

1. Why must so many bypass their churches in order to carry on effective ministry?
2. How long can a parachurch organization effectually minister to its clientele?

Let's take a further look at each of these questions.

At the time of conversion, God calls each of us to do those good works He has already prepared for us to do. To accept that call, we shouldn't have to bypass our local church. If we have ministry potential—and we all do—we shouldn't be confined to our pews on Sunday mornings; instead we should be encouraged to reach out to a hurting world. If God is at work within each of us, giving us the will and power to achieve His purpose, then we shouldn't have to go to an outside group to perform our ministry. That's why I urge clergy and laity alike to do away with the fortress mentality.

The local churches owe much to the working examples of the parachurch organizations.[3] We would all do well to become acquainted with and study the methodology and structure by which they are operated.

But "para" organizations are limited as to what they can offer. And while we can appreciate their work, we dare not underestimate our own potential to offer what they offer and more.

The Church has an important advantage over the para organizations. For one thing, we are the local visible functioning Body of Christ. Right off the bat that fact gives us authority and credibility. It also gives us a solid base from which to reach out to the masses. And most importantly, we offer total ministry, from the babes in arms to the aged senior citizen. Once people have been helped by a para organization, the transition from that group to the Church can be difficult, and many never make it. How much better if their needs had been met within a body of local believers.

It's safe to say that one of the reasons para ministries tend to be so successful is that they have the luxury of specializing. They have a built-in limited intent. For example, Youth for Christ doesn't try to minister to young children or young adults. All of their time, energy and resources can be spent on teenagers.

But this specialization can also create a serious problem. For once the person they are ministering to has his or her needs met, that person faces a difficult transition problem for the next stage of life. The local church, a body composed of all types of people of all ages, on the other hand, can fill the lifelong needs of an individual.

ONE MORE TIME!

Our culture's biggest need is for the very gospel message and value system our churches have to offer. To meet that need, the local church—the visible manifestation of the Body of Christ—is ordained by God to be His witness, to be salt and light to the world. But, in too many instances, we have abrogated our responsibility to a needy world and have turned inward, ministering only to ourselves. Consequently, the ministries that take place in the church are just not enough, if we are to fulfill the Great Commission. We must take our ministries from the fortress to the front lines.

How?

1. Put aside our fortress mind-set and stop boxing in our lay people and pastors.
2. Get outside the four walls of our churches and into the streets of our cities.
3. Look for groupings of people and design ministries with their life-styles in mind.
4. Entrust the lay people in our churches with ministry. They have tremendous ministry potential, can be trusted with ministry and will develop a "let's go after them" response, as God leads them into ministry and gives them a vision for it.
5. Recognize that guidance is available; books are written and conferences are held on how to get the laity involved in meaningful ministry, enabling us to benefit from the wisdom and experience of others already involved.
6. Employ our facilities as home base for major decen-

tralized ministries that develop as our people are unleashed into the city.
7. Believe that God, as He leads us into further ministry, can be trusted to supply necessary facilities and finances.

THE CHOICE IS OURS

In short, we have a choice: We can either target-group the city and get back in touch with the other two-thirds of our population, or we can carry on business as usual with the shrinking middle class.

What is our choice?

EXPLORING YOUR POTENTIAL

1. On a scale of 1 to 10 how would you rate your church?

1	2	3	4	5	6	7	8	9	10

Very
Fortress-minded

Not at All
Fortress-minded

2. List the types of ministries in which your church is currently involved.

3. What ministries are you personally taking part in? What needs do these ministries address?

4. Are there areas of ministry you'd like to explore? Name them and tell why.

Notes
1. Halverson voices this theme in his book, *The Timelessness of Jesus Christ,* published by Regal Books of Ventura, California (1982).
2. David McKenna, *Megatruth: The Church in the Age of Information* (San Bernardino, CA: Here's Life Publishers, 1987), p. 151.
3. A listing of many parachurch organizations is included at the back of this book.

CHAPTER 2

Taking Our Ministries to the Streets

When we consider unleashing the ministry potential of God's people, we need to consider the following question: How can Christians work out their potential if the work of our churches is restricted to the limited programs happening within the walls of the church?

In his book, *How I've Changed My Thinking About the Church*,[1] Richard Halverson, chaplain of the U.S. Senate, discusses how he began to see that most of the work of church people is to be centered outside the walls of the church. In *The Timelessness of Jesus Christ*, he continues that theme:

> The work of the church is outside the establishment. Outside the church. In the world. And it takes every member to do it! Nowhere in the Bible is the world exhorted to "come to

church." But the church's mandate is clear: She
must go to the world.[2]

This statement is not a put-down of those who minister faithfully within the walls of their church. No one is
more important in the kingdom than the faithful Sunday
School teacher, youth worker or worship leader. If you
talk to 10 young people who have committed themselves
to foreign missionary service, I would guess not many
were converted on the street or in jail. No, the vast majority of them are likely to have become Christians in Sunday
School, at vacation Bible school or at summer youth camp.

Those who minister in the traditional ministries of the
Church are crucial in the work of God's kingdom. But the
larger the congregation the smaller the percentage of people who will be needed for the internal ministries. What
does that leave the much larger percentage of believers
doing?

REACHING OUT MAKES A DIFFERENCE

A few years ago I was shocked when I heard that our state
of Colorado dealt with 176 cases of child abuse in 1971. A
decade later that number skyrocketed to over 10,000
cases.

Shortly after hearing those statistics, I arranged for
the head of Denver Social Services, in the area of child
abuse, to come to our church. Before that meeting I
shared the child abuse numbers with our congregation and
invited those interested in learning more to be there the
following Monday evening to meet with the representa-
tive. Over 300 people returned to hear what the social
worker had to say, and between 50-60 signed up, took

training and became special friends to either the children who had been abused or to their parents. This was the beginning of a specialized ministry in our church called The Care Company.

Come with me if you will to a Care Company support group meeting. Imagine that we are meeting in one of the volunteer worker's homes. We have met to share our ideas, the victories and the defeats we've experienced while working with our clients. And we have met to pray together.

We begin our time by going around the circle and reporting to the others about our ministry. The following are actual reports[3] from some Care Company volunteers. They tell the story of some who have taken their ministry to the streets.

Lauree and Isabelle

Lauree describes her relationship with 6-year-old Isabelle: "She sees me as a big sister and I feel that I'm about the only positive female influence in her life. The family is poor, but seem to have its basic needs met. The neighborhood is very bad for a small girl to grow up in. Isabelle lives with her father who is 'religious,' but I'm not sure if he is a true Christian. I'd really like to have an impact on the whole family."

Jim and Keith

Jim talks about his work with Keith, age 14. "We have an excellent relationship. Keith is very open and just needs someone to take an interest in him and consider him valuable. We've done various activities together such as skiing, movies, hiking, helping each other with housework and just talking. Keith needs love and self-acceptance. He has accepted Jesus. The seed was planted before I met him, but not watered or cared for. He needs continued comfort and encouragement."

Greg, Laurie and Chris

Greg and Laurie say of Chris, age 13: "His needs are many. The main people in his life don't have a clue about what's right and wrong. Nutrition and hygiene are poor; warm clothing is lacking. His mother doesn't understand his needs. She needs help with discipline and is much too severe with the children. She yells at them for anything. Her boyfriend occasionally beats them or locks them up. Mother is not independent enough to oppose her boyfriend."

If you're not pastor of your church, a Sunday School teacher or otherwise actively involved in another type of home-base ministry, maybe God is calling you to take your ministry to the streets.

Penny and Helen

Penny works with a young black/Hispanic woman, age 23, by the name of Helen. Penny has taken Helen to lunch, on picnics in the park and the mountains, for job hunting, to court hearings and out to dinner. "We are friends. I am her sounding board, her teacher and her substitute mother. I'm praying for her salvation and for guidance in leading Helen into God's Word."

Jerry and Jim

Jerry shares concerning 14-year-old Jim: "It has been a close relationship of sharing and helping each other. We go camping, sailing, horseback riding and play tennis together. Jim needs tutoring, encouragement and medical help with hyperactivity."

Marilyn and Michelle

The two-way learning experience of being a Care Company volunteer is noted by Marilyn: "I'm working with 7-year-old Michelle. She is learning to do many things; I am too! I'm developing a good relationship with her mom too. One week after spending time with Michelle, I went with her mom to help bail out a friend from jail. This has been an eye-opening experience for me.

"People are hurting and have real needs that can be met—a ride somewhere, a friend to talk to. Through Michelle, I have met some of her friends who are also in need of a big sister. They tell me the waiting list is long. The need is great!"

And the list goes on. I guarantee you, after sitting in on such a meeting, you will go away saying, This is not the time for Christians to be hiding away inside the walls of their churches. They need to be taking their ministry potential to the streets.

ARE YOU WILLING TO REACH OUT?

We live in a culture up for grabs, and one way for Christians to penetrate the world is to work with various social service agencies that are crying for volunteers. A typical commitment in this type of ministry is to spend three hours a week with your "client."

While a few are called to teach Sunday School, God may be calling thousands of Christians to become special friends to abused children. If the potential in our churches could be unleashed we could greatly ease the plight of abused children everywhere. And not only would we be alleviating some of the hurt caused by this scourge in our country, but we could also introduce scores of people to a personal relationship with Christ.

Would you be willing to reach out to children like the ones we've just discussed? Are there others in your church who might be interested in forming a Care Company just like the one at Bear Valley Church?

Our adversary the devil will work relentlessly to keep us boxed in and comfortable within the walls of our churches. He doesn't want Christ to touch lives of little ones like Isabelle or Keith or Michelle.

A certain number need to spend much of their time ministering inside the church walls. They have been called by God to a "home base" ministry. Are you one who has been called for just such a ministry? Or is your time in the temple dominated by listening to others teach or manage the plant and operation?

If you're not the pastor of your church, a Sunday School teacher or otherwise actively involved in another type of home-base ministry, maybe God is calling you to take your ministry to the streets.

EXPLORING YOUR POTENTIAL

1. How do you feel about the statement: "The Church's mandate is clear: She must go to the world"?

2. While the Church is admonished to go outside its fortress walls, the work of the faithful ministries going on inside the walls are valuable beyond measure. What part have the ministries inside the walls played in your Christian walk?

3. Can you think of some young people in your church or neighborhood who could use a support team like the Care Company described in this chapter?

4. Do you have any social workers in your church? If so, how can you be supportive of them? Has anyone in your church explored the possibilities of linking up a Care Company-type ministry with local social service agencies? How about you? Could you take the lead in forming a Care Company?

Notes
1. Richard Halverson, *How I Changed My Thinking About the Church* (Grand Rapids: Zondervan Publishing House, 1972), p. 71-79.
2. ———. *The Timelessness of Jesus Christ* (Ventura, CA: Regal Books, 1982), p. 104.
3. The names of individuals have been changed to protect their privacy.

CHAPTER 3

It Can Be Done in the Average Local Church

Bear Valley Church is not situated in the most ideal place for church growth. Although we are located on a main street, all the new growth in our part of the city is taking place a considerable distance to the south and west of us.

I'm not aware of any churches in the near north or east of our location that are growing or have grown in the past decade. Our part of the city was a new suburban area 30 years ago; it's not part of the city where much church growth is expected.

I like the fact that we're not in a place for easy growth. While I'm not opposed to large church facilities, I like the size of our church building. Our total space, including offices, is approximately 9,500 square feet and we sit on one acre of land. We may buy more land and build bigger facilities in the future, for any church should always keep its facility options open, but I'm pleased that up to now, no one can point to a choice location or huge facility to explain the growth and dynamics of the ministry that's taking place at Bear Valley Church.

Many churches in America have as good a setting and facilities to work with as we have. When it comes to the American suburban church, we are pretty average. The

---

Today, God's New Testament people need to experience that same godly confidence that resulted when Nehemiah prayed, lived a holy life, had confidence in God's Word and was creative in his thinking . . . . We have the people resources to do it! But we don't have the creative mind-sets.

---

secret for massive ministry penetration lies not in a handful of super churches, but in thousands of average churches just like Bear Valley and probably just like yours.

THINKING: THE MISSING INGREDIENT

Since becoming a Christian I've come to realize that wherever serious Christians gather, we can anticipate being challenged in the areas of Bible study, prayer and holy living. I call these Christian concerns The Big Three. And, despite the attention we give them, most of us feel we have a long way to go to reach a significant level of maturity in any of the three.

Yet, even though none of us has mastered The Big Three, I suggest that serious Christians need to add a fourth virtue: thinking. I'm confident that thousands of average churches exist with average locations and modest facilities just like ours. And the people in these churches are sincere about Bible study, prayer and holy living. But they are not seriously committed to thinking.

Week after week they are challenged to grow in The Big Three. Yet their churches remain static, lacking the missing dynamic that only front-line ministries can produce. Sensing that lack of dynamic, sincere leaders urge the flock to prayer even harder, to spend more time in Bible study and to live purer lives. But the Church continues to remain static and ingrown.

What is needed is to retain the emphasis on The Big Three, and to add the spark of thinking. Everyone, not just the elders, needs to have permission to think. Why? Because people in churches generally are conditioned to assume that "somebody up there is doing all the necessary thinking." Yet, when everyone is encouraged to think, the other three areas invariably come alive. Instead of mechanical prayer and Bible study, we then have dynamic prayer and study of the Word.

And what are people free to think about?

They are free to think about God, the beauty of life— and particularly about how God might use them as ambassadors to a hurting world. They are free to think about justice, mercy and the terror of spending an eternity in hell. More than that, they are free to think about how they might make a difference, for God has called them to something as significant as that to which He has called the missionary or the preacher.

Yes, we have a lot to think about!

Nehemiah: A Thinking Leader

Numerous books have been written about Nehemiah in recent years. They inevitably point out that Nehemiah was a thinking leader. He came to Jerusalem with a plan and a vision to rebuild the wall and, as a result, he instilled in God's people a godly confidence. And in 52 days they rebuilt their wall. They did it!

Interestingly, when Nehemiah challenged them, he said, "'You see the trouble we are in: Jerusalem lies in ruins, and its gates have been burned with fire. Come, let

---

The average Christian in the average church must accept the challenge for ministry. We simply cannot continue to depend on one church in 30 or 40 to have strong impacting ministries. We need to expect the majority of the churches to get involved.

---

us rebuild the wall of Jerusalem, and we will no longer be in disgrace.' I also told them about the gracious hand of my God upon me and what the king had said to me" (2:17-18).

Later in chapter 3, we see he had a plan, a way to get everybody involved in the project.

Today, God's New Testament people need to experience that same godly confidence that resulted when Nehemiah prayed, lived a holy life, had confidence in God's Word and was creative in his thinking. We live in days of unusual opportunity. There is not a sector of our culture that cannot be effectively penetrated with the gospel. We could befriend every international student, build bridges to every unchurched senior adult, link up with every abused child in the social services systems. We have the people resources to do it! But we don't have the creative mind-sets.

The average Christian in the average church must

accept the challenge for ministry. We simply cannot continue to depend on one church in 30 or 40 to have strong impacting ministries. We need to expect the majority of the churches to get involved.

We've discovered at our modest Denver location that people don't dwell on the fact we are facility poor when they are directly involved in ministry to others. Therefore, our primary concern over the years has not been the size or location of our facility, but rather how can we get people on the front-lines of ministry and keep them there.

A PLACE FOR DREAMERS

Several years ago a song entitled "California Dreamin'" was popular. Maybe evangelicals need to write a song called "Ministry Dreamin'."

Unfortunately, churches do not have a good track record in creating and unleashing dreamers. Too often new ideas and approaches to ministry are discouraged.

I received a letter recently from a man who said his pastor, after attending one of my seminars, apologized to his church for throwing wet blankets on their ideas for new ministries. He then told the church—to the delight of the man who wrote the letter—that from now on he would encourage everyone to dream about the possibilities of their church.

Yes, it's time to expect more of our churches. In too many cases, the average church is likely to focus on what it doesn't have, like a prime location, great facilities or top-notch programs for every age group. When that's the case the atmosphere becomes a defensive one focused on survival. Instead, the average church and its members need to create an atmosphere where people—leaders and laity alike—can dream dreams of ministry with the primary objective to glorify God and to enable every person to be at maximum in their own spiritual growth and ministry to others.

THE AVERAGE CHURCH HAS ENORMOUS POSSIBILITIES

Over the years dreamers in our church have been used by God to conceive, establish and run a host of ministries. Lay people envision the objective, devise the training, do the recruiting and direct the ministry. As long as they do not get into moral or doctrinal trouble and don't ask for money, we—the Bear Valley pastors and deacons—leave them alone.

In that rather freewheeling climate, a street school, medical clinic, Christian mediation service and ministries in the following areas have developed: step-families, cults, jail, street, refugees, senior adults, physically disabled, alcoholics and more.

Bear Valley is not unique. Several other churches around the country also have multiple and diverse ministries. But percentage-wise, such churches are too few in number. Yet we could increase their number. For the average church can produce multiple ministries, if the average people in them will pray, study Scripture, live holy lives *and* think and dream dreams.

A POSSIBLE SCENARIO

Why don't you begin to dream right now? Ask God for a burden and a vision for a particular ministry. Maybe God will lead you to one of the already established ministries in the church, or maybe He will lead you to direct your church into a new ministry.

The first step is to pray and confirm the desire in your heart. If you're pursuing a brand new ministry, the second step will be to begin to share the vision informally. Talk

---

If a church retains an average atmosphere where people are expected to pray, read the Bible and live holy lives, but are not encouraged to think or dream, then forget it. Not much is likely to happen. In fact, that average church is likely to remain average, and that's pretty sad when you think about it.

---

about what God has put on your heart and see if He has given others a similar burden.

If you sense there's enough interest to call a formal meeting, go to your pastor and share your vision. Remember, don't expect the church leadership to necessarily finance your ministry, design it or recruit for it. Pastors usually have their hands full. We have a saying at Bear Valley when it comes to starting and running ministries: "In this navy every tub sails on its own bottom." Don't ask your pastor to do it. Instead, seek his or her blessing and encouragement.

The next step will be to set your initial meeting and announce to the church that anyone interested in establishing a certain ministry is invited to attend. At that meeting, a number of things could happen. For example, no one could show up. If that's the case, God may be saying not now. You may need to try again later. If several show up, it's a good sign there's potential for this type of ministry. It's time to brainstorm and select leadership from those present. It may be obvious that someone else will make the best leader. That has to be okay. Sometimes God gives one person the vision and another the potential for leadership.

In our church only those interested in being part of the ministry are welcome at these initial meetings. In fact, it's terribly important that no pastors or elders show up, unless they are going to participate. Why? you ask. Because when someone with credentials shows up, the meetings lose their creativity. Often, with an authority figure present, the rank and file will not share their thoughts. Inevitably, too, the pastor becomes the focal point of the questions. And we pastors have been trained to give answers, whether we have them or not!

You see, by involving "official" church leaders who are not themselves active participants, the danger is that of creating ministries dependent on the pastors' oversight. And doing that will result in two things: (1) cripple the potential of lay people to be full-fledged leaders themselves, and (2) limit the number of ministries in a church to only those the pastors or elders can personally oversee.

Now, let's suppose 10 people show up for the first meeting, and five of them decide this venture is not for them. Then the following week, the five who are still on board need to regather and begin to make ministry plans and commitments. Hopefully, once the ministry is born, the church will advertise and encourage it. The process need not be complicated.

Whatever occurs at the initial meetings, leave the results to the Holy Spirit.

But nothing is likely to happen if average people in average churches remain preoccupied with what they don't have, instead of what they could have. If a church retains an average atmosphere where people are expected to pray, read the Bible and live holy lives, but are not encouraged to think or dream, then forget it. Not much is likely to happen. In fact, that average church is likely to remain average, and that's pretty sad when you think about it.

So what happens when average Christians begin to think and dream of ministry?

Here's one example: Several years ago some Christian mothers in Denver dreamed about a specialized ministry to *M*others *of P*reschooler*s*, and today MOPS is touching the lives of thousands of moms, children and whole family units (see chap. 8).

These mothers were average women in an average church who weren't afraid to dream. Then working to make their dream happen, they stopped being average; they became exceptional.

And God gave them an exceptional ministry!

EXPLORING YOUR POTENTIAL

1. How would you compare your church facilities to the facilities at Bear Valley Church?

2. Do you feel confident that you and your church have God's permission to have effective ministries other than those expected in most every church? Explain your answer.

3. If the sky were the limit, what kind of ministry would you like to be involved in?

4. What facilities outside your local church could be used for ministry? Be creative.

PART TWO
Discovering Your Potential

CHAPTER 4

Everyone Is Needed on the Wall

Nehemiah 3 is one of the rare biblical chapters that is both the most boring and the most important portion of the commentary on the rebuilding of Jerusalem's wall. It's *boring* because it's simply a list of people with hopeless-to-pronounce Jewish names and a location description of where they worked on the wall. It's *important* for two reasons.

First, this chapter lets us know that everyone got involved in the rebuilding project. And, second, it reminds us how diverse those people were: goldsmiths, perfume makers, district rulers, half-district rulers, Levites, priests, guards, merchants and dozens who are simply called "the son of."

We need to remember that when Nehemiah arrived on the scene in Jerusalem, the people had lived there with the wall in rubble for 80 years. And in only 52 days the wall was rebuilt!

How could such a dramatic turn-around take place? Because the people, under the leadership of Nehemiah, felt a fresh sense of godly confidence and everyone got involved.

Nehemiah knew the task he faced was too big and the situation was too dangerous for a long, drawn-out rebuilding campaign. He needed everyone involved and that's just what he got.

When we consider the Great Commission, we recognize that we are called to a task that's too big, much too big for a handful of professional clergy. The world's population is growing at a startling rate. Demographic experts project that the global population will grow from the 1984 figure of 4,762 million to 6,300 million by the year 2000. This means that the challenge to obey the Great Commission grows bigger by 200,000 people every day! That we must have everyone on the wall is obvious.

The popular author and conference speaker Howard Hendricks expressed the situation this way: "I tell you the truth, if we are waiting for the professionals to get this job done, the world's going to go to hell in a hatbox, because God never intended for it to be done that way."[1]

The idea of every Christian being a minister is nothing new. In fact, that idea has probably been the most repeated concept in dozens of church renewal and church growth books. One of the early renewal writers who has greatly influenced me is Elton Trueblood. Twenty years ago he wrote, "The more we study the early church, the more we realize that it was a society of ministers." He later added in the same writing, "At last we are beginning to see that it is the ordinary member who has the program and the pastor is his helper."[2]

Scores of other books like *Liberating the Laity* by R. Paul Stevens, *Layman Look Up* by Walt Henrickson and Gill Garrison, and more recently *Can the Pastor Do It Alone?* by Melvin J. Steinbron are typical of those written on this same subject.

Yet some 20 years after Trueblood's *Incendiary Fellowship*, the idea that every member is a minister has still not caught on. Why not?

The greatest thing leadership can do is let those they are leading grow to maturity . . . . How sad to see in the Church people who have been Christians for several years who do not have the confidence to minister to others.

The answer is complex. Yet without going into too much historical and sociological study I think I can offer a few good answers:

1. Most of our local churches have leadership, both clergy and lay, who do not provide visionary motivation.

2. Many of our leaders form parent-child relationships with their members, rather than collegial relationships.

3. There is still the illusion in most of our churches that formal classroom training must precede doing ministry. This type of false thinking produces clergy who tend to be condescending.

4. In too many instances, laity view a paid pastor as a hired gun to be "the minister" for the whole church.

5. Our churches generally lack the kind of strategy planning that would encourage everyone to be a minister.

We will discuss most of these reasons at length later on, but for now let's go back to Nehemiah and take a look at some who didn't get involved in rebuilding the wall.

THE NOBLES OF TEKOA

In Nehemiah 3:5 we read: "The next section was repaired by the men of Tekoa, but their nobles would not put their shoulders to the work under their supervisors."

Unfortunately, as in Nehemiah's day, nearly every church today has its nobles of Tekoa. For one reason or another they refuse to put their shoulders to the task at hand. And all too often they are influential enough to set the tone for the majority of the church.

Over the years our church has entered into joint ventures with several other congregations that have invited us to send pastors and lay people to help them rebuild their struggling churches. One such assembly was down to a handful of people. Their pastor intended to leave when he finished seminary and the whole church was thoroughly discouraged.

Since he was leaving, the pastor approached us about a joint venture. We worked out an arrangement agreeable to both churches in which one of our pastors and about 70 of our people joined up with their congregation, which by now was down to about a dozen members. You can imagine the impact of this large influx of people. Overnight the church began to grow. Children's programs came alive as did the youth and music ministries. The auditorium, which seated 150, was nearly full for the first time in years. Needless to say, the young pastor who took over the leadership of this church was perplexed when the nobles of Tekoa suddenly emerged.

Some Nobles Are Dead Weight

The oldest couple remaining from the original church began to complain. Here's what they had to say: (1) People walked right by them in the church foyer without greeting them; there was just too much hustle and bustle. (2) The Sunday School teacher used an overhead projector and had skits in their class; Sunday School should be a place where Bible is taught in pure lecture form. (3) The new people from Bear Valley didn't say amen during the preaching.

The young pastor was stunned. Couldn't the couple see the enormous amount of positive things happening in the church, which had been essentially rescued from the grave? Why their seemingly petty concerns?

Nobles from Tekoa are a fact of life. In Nehemiah's day all of Jerusalem felt a fresh wave of enthusiasm to rebuild the wall. But the nobles of Tekoa simply wouldn't get involved.

Tekoan nobles are still around today and can end up playing two different roles in our churches; they can actively impede or passively become mere spectators. This couple in our example managed to do both. Before Bear Valley and their church entered the joint venture, they crippled their church with their negative attitudes. Finally, during the process of working out the joint venture, they relinquished their former position of calling the shots to becoming little more than dead weight.

Some Nobles Control the Power Structure

While some nobles are just dead weight, the most destructive ones control the formal or informal power structures. I saw such a situation a few years back when a creative pastor wanted to start alternate-style congregations in his church. The church was full in their Sunday services, and they either needed to build or begin multiple congregations.

In the process of discussing change, some of the people in the church wanted to start this proposed service with its different flavor. Another pastor friend of mine was invited to attend the church business meeting where the topic of this alternate style was discussed. He later told me the whole atmosphere was explosive. The people who wanted the change sat on one side of the room, while the opposition sat on the other.

When the smoke finally cleared, the Tekoan nobles had their way. They successfully blocked the attempt by those who wanted to experiment with an alternate congregation.

That's the tragedy of Tekoan nobility in the power structure of a church. They resist any kind of change, risk or experimentation. They normally want to keep things small and static so they can maintain control. Left to themselves such nobles of Tekoa can be a deadly force and can eventually kill a church.

Fortunately, for Nehemiah and for Jerusalem, the Tekoan nobles in chapter 3 were not in the power structure, they were just dead weight. They didn't block the attempt of others to respond to the challenged, they just didn't get involved.

LEADERSHIP DETERRENTS TO LAY MINISTRY

Many churches never have the opportunity to find out if they possess anyone other than Tekoan-type nobles. They never find out because their leadership never seriously challenges anyone to get involved as ministers. Sure, they may occasionally preach that everyone is a minister, but nothing ever happens.

The paid leadership in many churches often gives the

laity a double message. Verbally, they say everyone can be a minister. But their style of leadership communicates they don't want their laity to think of themselves as ministers.

Determining the reasons for this mixed message could get very involved, and the purpose for this book is to encourage laity to unleash their potential to be ministers and for the clergy to encourage them to do so. Therefore, we will make only brief comments in this area.

Paternal Leadership

For three consecutive summers a man visited our church; he lived elsewhere during the winter months (smart man). At the close of his final summer, he invited my wife and me out to dinner. During the course of the evening's conversation, he really got my attention when he commented, "I think I know the genius of the ministry in your church."

I was obviously eager to hear more, so he continued. "You treat people like you expect them to be mature."

That was it? Just 10 brief words? I was expecting, or at least hoping for, something a bit more profound.

That conversation took place several years ago. But I think about it often and the more I do, the more profound it becomes.

Over the years I have made a deliberate attempt not to take on a father image as pastor. I don't want to be a parent to hundreds of people. In the first place, I doubt I could be a very good parent figure to the church. And second, I'm afraid that if I try to parent our church, many will allow me to do so, and they won't have to grow up!

The greatest thing leadership can do is let those they are leading grow to maturity. The only way children will ever mature and reach their potential as adults is for their parents to allow them to grow up. How sad it is to see 30- or 40-year-old men and women still relating in childish, immature ways toward their parents. Normally, when that happens it's because the parents themselves refused to treat their children in a mature way. How sad to see in the Church people who have been Christians for several years who do not have the confidence to minister to others.

Overly Academic Leadership

Could it be that we vocational clergy often struggle to allow the laity to be genuine ministers because we often are personally insecure? Or maybe it has to do with the type of training we have received. Most pastors have been through college and seminary, where we've spent long hours wrestling with academic issues. And for the most part that's good; there is no virtue in uneducated leaders.

Lay people in most churches seem too content just to hire people to do the ministry work that needs to be done. It's easier to pay someone else than to commit themselves to get involved . . . a hired-gun mentality.

But the enormous overbalance toward the academic and conceptual is not healthy. Perhaps you've heard that professional academicians in the Middle Ages spent hours debating such burning questions as, How many angels can dance on the head of a pin? I must confess, in my seven years of classroom education beyond high school, I heard many "pinhead" type discussions.

Condescending Leadership

The fact that the vocational leadership in the church is normally trained in hot-house academic settings has several implications for the local church. One such implication is that it's easy for professional clergy to be condescending toward laity.

Professionally trained pastors are often afraid to release lay people into ministry because they haven't had the academic training we have had. We're convinced the laity won't do things right, especially if their ministry requires them to do any serious teaching. We pastors tend to forget that people are intelligent and have access to incredible educational resources without getting formal training. But pastors often pick up a spirit from their former professors that "no one really knows this subject like we do." And, subconsciously, we tend to carry that mentality into our pastorates.

THE LAITY: "LET THE PASTOR DO IT!"

The vocational clergy however are not the only ones who have mind-sets hindering the "everyone is a minister" idea. Lay people in most churches seem too content just to hire people to do the ministry work that needs to be done. It's easier to pay someone else than to commit themselves to get involved.

I often talk with discouraged pastors who sincerely want to equip lay people to minister. They really want to see people unleashed into ministry. But the lay people in their church operate with a hired-gun mentality. And in too many instances, laity feel too insecure to think of themselves as ministers. After all, they "have neither much ministry experience nor any formal theological training."

UNTRAINED, BUT WILLING TO
MAKE A DIFFERENCE

One woman named Carol wanted to join the team of jail lay workers. She began a Tuesday evening Bible study for women inmates. On any given Tuesday evening, Carol would have a half dozen women or so join her. One night, however, only one woman showed up for study. Since there were just the two of them, Carol seized the opportunity to know more about Rebecca. The story Carol heard, while not unusual to hear in a jail setting, shook her.

When Rebecca's mother was expecting her, the father couldn't stand his wife being pregnant and tried to shoot her. In self-defense Rebecca's mother shot him. As a young girl Rebecca continually heard that her father hadn't wanted her. Then when she was seven, her mother shot herself in front of Becky. For the next three years, she lived with relatives, where she was sexually abused. At the tender age of 10, Rebecca hit the streets and started using drugs.

As Rebecca shared her story, Carol asked the Lord for the wisdom to respond correctly. The study she had prepared for that evening no longer seemed appropriate. For a moment, Carol regretted having taken the risk to minister in the jail. What could she say to Rebecca? Then the Lord brought to mind the story of the biblical Rebecca. As Carol related that story, she emphasized the fact that the Old Testament Rebecca had made a decision to obey God and walk with Him.

That evening a modern-day Rebecca made that same choice. From then on Rebecca became Carol's most enthusiastic student, and often took the new truths she was learning from Scripture back to the other inmates.

In time one of Rebecca's cellmates, Janita, wanted to know how she too could invite Christ into her life. Although Rebecca did not know a lot of Scripture, she did know that Carol had introduced her to Christ through the story of her Old Testament namesake. So Rebecca gave Carol a call and asked, "Are there any Janitas in the Bible? I have a friend by that name who wants to invite Jesus into her life."

One thing led to another and, in spite of the fact there are no Janitas in the Bible, she too committed her life to Christ.

Carol was not only involved in the jail ministry of Bear Valley, she also wanted to be part of our creative outreach team. Creative outreach is a ministry that conducts various evangelistic events, the main ones being dinner parties in country clubs or very nice restaurants.

Carol invited her boss and his wife to one such dinner. At the conclusion of the dinner, the wife checked on her decision card that she wanted to become a Christian. The husband also indicated an interest. Carol was thrilled at their response, since they were both Hindus from India. Her boss is a Ph.D. and very influential in the Indian association in the Denver area.

Besides inviting her boss to the dinner party, Carol gave him a copy of C.S. Lewis's *Mere Christianity*. As she will tell you herself, she is not an especially gifted person, nor does she have any formal Bible or theological training. But she does have access to resources, such as *Mere Christianity* and other similar works. Perhaps Carol's greatest credential for ministry is her vision and desire to be used of God; she isn't looking for a hired-gun pastor to do the ministry for her.

Prior to coming to our church, Carol had been involved in several churches as a Sunday School teacher and a choir member, two vital ministries. But it never occurred to Carol then that she could ever be used in a jail or dinner party ministry. Carol, like thousands of capable lay

---

Actually, for the vast majority of ministries you don't need a lot of special training. What you most need is a sincere desire to minister and touch others with the love of Jesus Christ.

---

people, had never been part of a Christian community that believed in her enough to release her into new spheres of ministry.

Carol and others like her not only touch lives for Christ, they also provide a model for other nonprofessional ministers who generally tend to underestimate their own ability to minister, while at the same time expecting too much of the paid clergy.

If you ask the average Christian whether he or she feels qualified to have a ministry, this is what you might hear in reply: "But I haven't been to seminary and haven't studied Greek! And what if someone raises a theological question I'm not prepared to answer?"

These feelings exist even though we are in the midst of an information explosion. Today's lay Christian has access to resources that surpass those available to even the professional clergy throughout most of the history of the Church. Books, tapes, videos, conferences—all are rich sources of information readily available. And for training in a specific ministry area, chances are good that you can obtain those needed resources as well.

Actually, for the vast majority of ministries you don't need a lot of special training. What you most need is a sincere desire to minister and touch others with the love of Jesus Christ. Most of the ministries we have in our church simply need people who will be special friends. International students, senior adults, physically disabled, prisoners, abused children—and the list goes on—primarily need someone who has Christ living in them to be a special friend, someone they can talk to and count on. If you can be a special friend to someone, you can be a minister.

WE NEED EVERYONE ON THE WALL

Nehemiah had room for everyone on the wall in his rebuilding the security of Jerusalem. And the Church today has room for everyone to minister in one way or another. Somehow in our churches, we must eliminate the reticence of our lay persons to serve. This reticence is caused by

- feelings of insecurity caused by a child/parent-type relationship with the clergy,
- attitudes of inadequacy because of "not enough training," and
- false assumptions brought on by leave-it-to-the-hired-gun mind-sets.

If Christ dwells within you, and you desire to be used in ministry, then many opportunities await you. I can't promise that all such opportunities will be exciting or will bring you much applause. But I can promise you the thrill of knowing that God is using you in a direct way to touch the lives of others. You can get involved on the wall, even

if you haven't been to an official brick-laying school.
   Yes, you too can be a minister!

EXPLORING YOUR POTENTIAL

1. Describe how you feel about the phrase, *everyone a minister.*

2. Describe what you believe is your church leadership's view of *everyone a minister.*

3. On the whole, would you say the laity in your church have the attitude, "Let the pastor do it!"

4. Are you like Carol in this chapter, not trained but willing? What resources are readily available for your use in sharing God's love with a lost and hurting world?

Notes

1. From the videotape, *Monday Morning Mission,* released by Harvest Communications, Wichita, Kansas.

2. Elton Trueblood, *The Incendiary Fellowship* (New York: Harper & Row, Publishers, Inc., 1967).

CHAPTER 5

Hearts in Tune with God's Heart

I'd been on the treadmill for only three minutes. Those three minutes seemed like an eternity. The year was 1971 and I was in my third year of seminary.

During those years of relentlessly exercising my brain, my body had literally gone to pot. The best way to describe my appearance was to say I looked something like a pregnant broom! I weighed 123 pounds and at nearly 5 feet, 11 inches, I was walking death with a little pot belly.

I not only looked terrible, I felt terrible. For years I had been working two and three jobs while trying to get through school and still be a decent husband and father. I just never took the time to exercise. And so there I was at age 31 trying to jog for three minutes on a treadmill, and nearly dying.

Since that time I have faithfully exercised. And today I'm a 150-pound pregnant broom—some things never change. Even though I've been jogging for several years, I still find it difficult. I hated running the day I stepped on that jogging machine and ran for three whole minutes, and I still struggle to keep up the discipline of jogging. But I like the idea of having a healthy heart.

Some of the deepest truths of the Christian faith can best be learned as we listen to the criticisms of our enemies. We evangelicals have a lot to learn about power structures, economics, prejudices and a host of other topics. But the most important thing we have to learn about is our own hearts.

I also like the idea of having a healthy heart spiritually. I will be eternally grateful that I was born into a spiritually disciplined Christian community. I was 22-years-old when I committed my life to Christ. The first year we were Christians, my wife Mary and I memorized 107 Bible verses through the Navigator's Topical Memory System. We had regular devotional times and we developed a consistent habit of reading and studying the Bible.

We continued to practice these disciplines while I was going through college, in spite of the pressures of raising a family. Like my struggle with jogging, I often didn't like getting up extra early to spend time with the Lord or disciplining my mind to remember a verse of Scripture. But I liked the results in my relationship with God.

All of Scripture was fresh and new to me. But the passages that spoke about the heart stood out in my mind. My college studies at Long Beach State spoke to my brain, but nothing had ever spoken to my heart like Scripture did.

MEN IN TUNE WITH GOD

One of the first verses I memorized even described my heart: "The heart is deceitful above all things and beyond cure. Who can understand it?" (Jer. 17:9). Then after God describes our hearts He lets us know that: "I the Lord search the heart and examine the mind, to reward a man according to his conduct, according to what his deeds deserve" (v. 10). One of the Proverbs I tucked away in memory was: "Above all else, guard your heart, for it is the wellspring of life" (4:23).

John Wesley

Shortly after I became a Christian, I entered college to pursue a degree in history. One of the figures I studied was John Wesley. Though my secular history course professor didn't spend much time on Wesley's life, I decided to study his life on my own. In his *Journal* I read the account of his conversion: "About a quarter before nine, while he (the leader of the meeting) was describing the change which God works in the heart through faith in Christ, I felt my heart strangely warmed."[1]

The outworking of Wesley's heartfelt conversion was, in my opinion, a demonstration of the type of ministry that results from a heart being in touch with God's heart.

Wesley's impact was felt throughout the British Isles. He preached in churches, in open fields and to coal miners. He influenced the beginning of the Sunday School, which originally began as a ministry to children factory workers, as well as ministries that came into existence a century after his death, such as the Salvation Army. Wesley had a heart that beat with God's heart and he impacted his turbulent era, as well as future generations.

I was making these discoveries about Wesley during my college days, 1963-1968. Because of the rioting of the '60s, I often had to drive through National Guard checkpoints to get to the campus. And once in class I was constantly challenged by the radicals of those days: Marxists, Black Power advocates and those espousing free sex and free (filthy) speech.

Some of the radicals had important and thought-provoking things to say. They spoke out on economics, power structures, racism and a host of other burning issues of the day. But they had nothing to say about the issue of the human heart. They saw rampant evil in their culture, but they were blind to the unrestrained evil in their own hearts.

So in that turbulent environment I learned what I could about power structures, economics, racism, prejudice, and much more. But both Mary and I committed ourselves to majoring on developing hearts that would beat with God's heart.

Now over two decades later, I'm grateful for the college days of the '60s. I'm glad I was forced to interact with all sorts of radicals. Tony Campolo expresses my sentiment so well in his book, *Partly Right:* "A religious group matures and improves only by correcting its flaws, and usually the enemies of that group can help it to see those flaws better than its friends can."[2] And that is true, not only for groups, but for individuals as well.

Some of the deepest truths of the Christian faith can best be learned as we listen to the criticisms of our enemies. We evangelicals have a lot to learn about power structures, economics, prejudices and a host of other topics. But the most important thing we have to learn about is our own hearts. Developing a heart that's in tune with God's heart is still life's highest achievement.

Nehemiah

The opening verses of the book bearing Nehemiah's name reveal that he was a passionate man, full of intense feelings. And it's also clear that his heart was in tune with God's heart. I suppose that's why I fell in love with this biblical character, Nehemiah, and have used him as an example throughout this book.

Many lay people out there in our churches today are burdened for the work that needs to be done. And these people are not necessarily among the trained clergy. They haven't been to bricklayer's school, but they can help rebuild the wall.

While still in Persia, Nehemiah heard that Jerusalem's wall was in rubble and the people were living amid great trouble and disgrace.

In Nehemiah's reaction to the news of Jerusalem's sorry state, we gain a glimpse into this man's heart. "When I heard these things, I sat down and wept. For some days I mourned and fasted and prayed before the God of heaven" (1:4).

When his brother told him of the mess in Jerusalem, Nehemiah could have said, "That's too bad, but tell me, Hanani, how about you? How are you doing?" Nehemiah could have shrugged the news off and gone on with his life. But instead, he immediately responded with weeping and mourning. Nehemiah was genuinely heartbroken.

And when you stop to think about it, God must have been heartbroken also. For Jerusalem was unique among the cities of the Old Testament. Certainly God is moved by any environment where people live in poverty, discouragement and disgrace. But in the Old Testament, He had a particular concern for Jerusalem. With Jerusalem destitute, we can be sure God's heart was broken in a special way. Nehemiah understood that, and his immediate reaction to the sad news revealed that his heart was broken too.

GOD'S GREAT COMMISSION STRATEGIES

God's Old Testament strategy for fulfilling the Great Commission was different from His strategy in the New Testament. In the New Testament era, God's strategy is to make Himself known through the witness of an international people called Christians. Christians are commanded to go and make disciples everywhere.

The Old Testament contains no such missionary mandate. God's strategy in the Old Testament was to make Himself known through the nation of Israel. And Israel's capital city had a significant role to play. That role included the presence of the Temple where God resided in a unique way, and the results of His rule would be on display to the nations.

As a result of its privileged relationship with their God, Israel was to be a national showcase for righteousness, justice and mercy. Just as the Olympics have become a place for nations to attempt to showcase the superiority of their systems and their athletes, so Israel, and Jerusalem in particular, was to showcase the superiority of Israel's God.

In 1 Kings 10:6-9, we see the Old Testament version of the Great Commission working at its best. Here, the Queen of Sheba, who came to visit King Solomon in Jerusalem, was impressed with the righteousness, justice, general welfare and happiness of the city's people. As a result she exclaimed to Solomon, "Praise be to the LORD your God" (v. 9). That's what was supposed to happen in Jerusalem. God's rule over His people was to be a powerful testimony to the nations.

All of this was common knowledge to the average Jew, just as the Great Commission to spread the gospel and make disciples everywhere is common knowledge to the average Christian. But unfortunately, knowledge without response is often all it is. For Nehemiah, God's plan for Jerusalem was more than a familiar truth. He had God's agenda *burning deeply in his heart.* And when Christians develop hearts that beat with God's heart, His agenda for fulfilling the Great Commission will be far more than mere common knowledge; we will act upon it.

NEEDED: MODERN NEHEMIAHS

Sadly, as the twentieth century closes, we see some parallels between the walls of Jerusalem in Nehemiah's day and the condition of many local churches today.

A friend of mine from another state stopped by recently to take me to lunch. As we caught up on the past couple of years, he shared with me that his church had just gone through a major split. The group that he was part of had left the church and was limping along, but holding its own. The group that stayed had suffered several more splits. Unfortunately, such depressing news as this is not uncommon. God's heart truly must be broken. Just as Jerusalem was crucial to God's great commission plan in the Old Testament, so the local church is crucial to His Great Commission plans in the New Testament.

In the pages of the New Testament, God's primary instrument—and some would argue *only* instrument—to carry out the Great Commission is clearly the local church. But in our day we have produced strong Christian schools, strong Christian publishing houses, hundreds of potent parachurch agencies and, in general, *weak churches*. I have worked with dozens of denominations in the past few years and, with very few exceptions, I find them generally discouraged over the condition of their churches. And God's heart is broken.

If the condition of our churches breaks God's heart, imagine how He feels about our society in general. Families are breaking up, children are being molested, prisons are overflowing, sex sin runs rampant. God's heart must truly be broken.

Where are our modern-day Nehemiahs? Where are the men and women whose hearts are in tune with God's heart?

I know where they are. I believe many lay people out there in our churches today are burdened for the work that needs to be done. And these people are not necessarily among the trained clergy. They haven't been to bricklayer's school, but they can help rebuild the wall.

I also believe many lay people need encouragement to realize they have what it takes to minister to the needs in this broken culture. And they need to know they can carry on their ministries with the support of their local church.

Of course, those people burdened to do God's work today but who find no support from their local church could always work out the unleashing of their ministry potential in some other context. They could pursue all that God has for them through the many parachurch organizations that are currently operating, or they could begin new parachurch organizations. But modern Nehemiahs always will have a heart for the local church. They will see the local church as Nehemiah saw Jerusalem: special to God and designed by Him to be the primary instrument in carrying out the Great Commission.

We may not like it, but our individual potential as Christians is dependent on the local body in which we function. Indeed, a few people have callings in life that do not make fellowship in a church possible. But 90 percent or more of us are intended by God to grow to our ministry potential in the context of a local church.

GOD'S DESIGN INCLUDES INTERDEPENDENCE

We need each other. The clergy and laity alike, young and old, need the love and support of one another. Have you ever wondered why the favorite scriptural analogy for the Church is a body? Granted, Scripture also provides other analogies; the Church is called a bride, a vineyard, a flock and a building. But more often than any of these His Church is called a body.

In 1 Corinthians, the apostle Paul laid out an extended analogy between the Church and a body. Paul wrote this letter to a particular church. In other words this analogy was not intended for the nebulous concept of the universal, invisible Church, but to instruct the visible local church at Corinth.

"The eye cannot say to the hand, 'I don't need you!' And the head cannot say to the feet, 'I don't need you!'

. . . Now you are the body of Christ, and each one of you
is a part of it" (1 Cor. 12:21,27).

The implication is clear. There is an interdependence
between the parts. The throwing arm of a great Hall of
Fame quarterback like Johnny Unitas may be highly
praised, but the arm had to depend on several other body
parts working together with it. If Unitas's eyes couldn't
see, it wouldn't have mattered how great his arm was.

Recently this truth came home to me in a fresh way. I
was talking with a man whose ministry is primarily with
athletes. He had just come from another city where he had
stayed in the home of a famous star of the National Bas-
ketball Association (NBA). He related that this ballplayer
was a relatively new Christian who needed to find a
healthy church home where the body of believers would
treat him as just another believer, not as a celebrity. My
friend who's had years of experience in parachurch ministries with athletes lamented that in such a context the
Christian athlete is treated as "the star." Most of these
athletes were stars in high school, college, the NBA or the
National Football League (NFL), and now they're stars in
a paraministry.

But stars need some place where they are just another
part of the body, a place where little old ladies could care
less if they scored 30 points the night before. These ladies
will want to know if these stars have written their mothers
lately and how they are treating their wives. Stars need little old ladies, and vice versa.

THE CURSE OF RUGGED INDIVIDUALISM

In America, with its great stress on individualism, we are
likely to overlook the fact that God has designed the Chris-

tian life to be lived corporately and interdependently. I have a fear that a theme like "unleashing your potential" may conjure up the idea of "my God and my potential," but that's not the idea here at all.

We may not like it, but our individual potential as Christians is dependent on the local body in which we function. In some cases that may not be a church. Through the jail ministry in our church, we're in touch with believers who are restricted to a fellowship of inmates. On a couple of occasions, I've spoken at chapels for professional football players. These believers spend several weeks of the year, during their playing years, in a fellowship situation that doesn't constitute a full-fledged local church.

Indeed, a few people have callings in life that do not make fellowship in a church possible. But 90 percent or more of us are intended by God to grow to our ministry potential in the context of a local church. And that won't be difficult if both clergy and laity are people whose hearts are in tune with God's heart.

Hearts that beat with God's heart will have a deep commitment to the local church, just as Nehemiah had for the welfare of Jerusalem. They will not see the local church as a place to maintain a handful of ministries for the middle class, but rather as God's primary commitment to reach all of culture.

EXPLORING YOUR POTENTIAL

1. What new steps can you take to develop a heart in tune with God's heart?

2. John Wesley is one of many whose heart was in tune with God's heart. In the annals of church history are many more just like him. Perhaps you'd like to pick an individual and do an in-depth study of that person's life.

3. The beginning of a ministry is a broken heart. As you look around, do you see areas of human ruin that break your heart? Would you consider a ministry in any of these areas?

4. Can you name some modern-day Nehemiahs in your church or community? Have you discovered your potential to be a modern-day Nehemiah?

Notes
1. John Wesley, *The Journal of John Wesley*   (Grand Rapids: Zondervan Publishing House, 1986), p. 64.
2. Tony Campolo, *Partly Right* (Waco, TX: Word Books, 1985), p. 9.

CHAPTER 6

You've Got Potential and Permission!

The woman on the other end of the phone asked a strange question, "Has your church ever considered running a state-licensed home for delinquent girls?"

It didn't take me long to confess the idea had never occurred to us. "But then," I answered, "we're always ready to listen to new ideas."

She said she and her husband had leased a house to the state, who in turn had used the facility as a group home for delinquent girls. But the operation had a history of staff problems. The state, it seems, could find people with the right academic credentials to run the home, but they had a difficult time coming up with staff who had the intangible qualities of good morals based on an absolute value system. Finally, after a number of problems between the staff and the girls, the state decided to close the home.

Since the couple were Christian, they felt the home could be reopened if they found a Christian agency to sponsor it. In the days following that phone call, some of us in the church began to investigate the possibility of our church becoming that Christian agency.

OPPORTUNITY PLUS FAITH

At first the obstacles seemed overwhelming. Initially there was the state to contend with. Would they license a Christian-run home for girls? Then would we be able to find qualified staff with the right academic credentials?

We also realized that an effective ministry with delinquent girls would require some highly committed volunteers in addition to the staff to work with the girls. And, as always, there was the problem of money.

Before we could submit a formal proposal, we knew it could take from six weeks to six months to get an answer. And during that time we would have to finance a facility and a staff. If the state delayed their response, the up-front money could be several thousands of dollars.

The needs were formidable, but God seemed to be putting the whole deal together. We decided to step out in faith and lease the home and hire the staff. It just so happened that a fellow in our church, who had a masters degree in social work, was looking for a job. We also found committed Christians with the right credentials for each of the other staff positions. With the house leased and staff hired, we submitted our proposal to the state.

The proposal made it clear that we intended to run the home with a Christian staff who would model Christian values. We were careful to make it clear that we had no intention of forcing our convictions on the girls. But we were honest about our desire to run a home that would have a Christian atmosphere.

There were many skeptics both inside and outside our church. They doubted the state would give us a license. And if we did get a license, those same skeptics were confident the "religion" question would delay the approval, forcing us to pay for a staff and a house for several months without any income.

Unleashing our churches and our potential for personal ministry means moving away from the world's fascination with titles and external credentials. The only title that really matters is the title of Christ-one. If you wear that title, you have authority as God's ambassador.

Fortunately for us our proposal was approved in the shortest time possible—six weeks—and we began our ministry with a good facility, a completely credentialed staff of Christians, plus several volunteer workers from the church.

We ran the home for four years before the state cut funding for all such homes. But during our years of operation we gained a great reputation with the state. They paid us over $1200 per girl per month and we ran an excellent home. There were times when every girl in the home had made a personal commitment to Christ. Committing their lives to Christ didn't solve all their problems, but once the girls had a reason for living, much of their deviant behavior subsided. Numerous relationships were established between people in our church and the girls. Some of those relationships continue to this day.

Delinquent girls are a tough bunch, and our kids were

no exception. But God engineered a way for us to minister to them. Our experience with the girls' home was a good one for the girls and a good one for our church. But if you had been in my office the morning we received that first call, I would have told you, "The woman has an intriguing idea, but I can't see any possible way we could even attempt to meet her request; we just don't have the resources."

GOD WILL SUPPLY THE RESOURCES

Not having the resources made us prime candidates to be used of God. Certainly Jesus' 12 disciples didn't appear to have much to offer. This memo to Jesus speaks volumes:

> To: Jesus, Son of Joseph
> Woodcrafters Carpenter Shop
> Nazareth 25922
> From: Jordan Management Consultants
> Jerusalem 26544
> Subject: Staff Team Evaluation
>
> Thank you for submitting the resumes of the twelve men you have picked for management positions in your new organization. All of them have now taken our battery of tests; and we have not only run the results through our computer, but also arranged personal interviews for each of them with our psychologist and vocational aptitude consultant . . . .
> It is the staff opinion that most of your nominees are lacking in background, education and vocational aptitude for the type of enterprise

you are undertaking. They do not have the team concept. We would recommend that you continue your search for persons of experience in managerial ability and proven capacity.

Simon Peter is emotionally unstable and given to fits of temper. Andrew has absolutely no qualities of leadership. The two brothers, James and John, the sons of Zebedee, place personal interest above company loyalty. Thomas demonstrates a questioning attitude that would tend to undermine morale. We feel it is our duty to tell you that Matthew has been blacklisted by the Greater Jerusalem Better Business Bureau. James, the son of Alphaeus, and Thaddaeus definitely have radical leanings, and they both registered a high score on the manic-depressive scale.

One of the candidates, however, shows great potential. He is a man of ability and resourcefulness, meets people well, has a keen business mind and has contacts in high places. He is highly motivated, ambitious and responsible. We recommend Judas Iscariot as your controller and right-hand man. All of the other profiles are self-explanatory.

We wish you every success in your new venture . . . . [1]

The first-century Church in which the apostles participated was a potent Church, yet Paul reminds the Corinthians: "Brothers, think of what you were when you were called. Not many of you were wise by human standards; not many were influential; not many were of noble birth" (1 Cor. 1:26).

When we consider Nehemiah we see that God is consistent. He operates the same way in the Old Testament as He does in the New Testament. Certainly if God were looking for a partner who has his own resources to rebuild Jerusalem's wall, Nehemiah was a poor choice. You name it, Nehemiah didn't have it.

CRUCIAL INGREDIENTS FOR MINISTRY

There are three crucial resources we need to do ministry. We need time, authority and materials. As a slave, Nehemiah didn't have any of these. The only thing he had was a broken heart.

A broken heart. A heart in tune with God's heart. Oh, Nehemiah had one other thing. He had access to the king, who had access to all the resources Nehemiah needed.

That should be encouraging to you, that is, if you have a broken heart, a heart in tune with God's heart. Because you too have access to the King! And the King has all the resources you will ever need to do anything!

All the Time We Need

"Then the king, with the queen sitting beside him, asked me, 'How long will your journey take, and when will you get back?' It pleased the king to send me; so I set a time" (Neh. 2:6).

The most important resource God has given us is time. When we're out of time, we're out!

Since becoming a believer, I've come to realize what a terrible thing it is to kill time. Sure, we need to stop and smell the roses every once in a while, but none of us has any time to kill.

Nehemiah had to ask the king for enough time to do the job and the king gave it to him. That's illustrative of how God operates. God didn't call Nehemiah to a three-year task and then give him only two years to do it. Likewise, God has given us all the time we need to accomplish our God-given tasks.

Often God wants to use our need for material resources to teach us vital lessons about our dependence on Him. Dependence, however, is not intended to foster worry, but rather to develop faith . . . . We can be confident that if we are seeking after God, He can and will supply all the necessary materials we need to do what work He has for us.

The Stewardship of Time. Since Nehemiah was a slave, he realized that his time was not his own. We, on the other hand, live as free men and women and often live with the illusion that time belongs to us. But of course, it doesn't; we are mere stewards of whatever time God has entrusted to us.

How much time is that? Obviously none of us know. Not even we Christians know how much time we have. We know we will live for eternity, but on temporal terms, we can't be certain we'll even be alive in the next minute. We can be sure of one thing, however: We have enough time to finish whatever our Lord has for us to do.

The Father gave Jesus just three and a half years for His public ministry. Nevertheless, Jesus says in John 17:4:

"I have brought you glory on earth by completing the work you gave me to do."

Our Lord's time was brief, but He was able to finish the task the Father had given Him. How much time we have doesn't matter; what does matter is that we have enough, but none to waste.

The Investment of Time. We all need to take a serious look at how we are investing our "church work" time. In one of his films, Dr. James Dobson reminds us that on the frontier if people missed a stage, they just waited another month for the next one. But today if we miss one section of a revolving door we have a nervous breakdown! We are doing our ministries in the pressure-packed world of the end of the twentieth century, not the slow-moving atmosphere of the rural frontier.

We have very limited amounts of time to invest directly into the work of the Church, and we need to be much more discriminating about how we use that limited time. I believe our churches are using way too much time managing things that do not warrant a big time investment. Peter Drucker once commented while speaking to a group of pastors, "One of the reasons church fights tend to be so big is that the stakes tend to be so small."

A second area of time use that we need to rethink is the number of meetings we expect "good" church members to invest time in. Presently, we expect people to attend Sunday School, Sunday morning and evening worship, Wednesday evening prayer meeting, regular Bible study and any number of committee meetings. No wonder so few people have any time left for investing in ministry beyond the walls of the church.

Remembering then that, of the three crucial resources we need to do ministry, the first is time, you need to ask yourself, How am I using my time? How well am I investing it? If you're going to be serious about ministry, maybe you don't have time for so many meetings, services, socials—even Bible studies.

All the Authority We Need

Next to time, Nehemiah asked for authority.

In His parable about the vine and the branches, Jesus made it clear that His followers are utterly and totally dependent on Him: "I am the vine; you are the branches. If a man remains in me and I in him, he will bear much fruit; apart from me you can do nothing" (John 15:5).

While we are totally dependent on Him, just as a branch is to the vine, we have access to the power of the vine.

This parable teaches us that authority is like time. We need not ask for more. If we are in Christ, we already have all we need. When it comes to time, we have enough; we just may not be investing very wisely. When it comes to authority, our Lord's authority is ours, we just may not have the faith to claim it or to walk in the necessary dependence.

The apostle Paul drove home his point about the believer and authority by telling the Corinthians, "We are ambassadors for Christ" (2 Cor. 5:20, *NASB*). When he addressed them as ambassadors he wasn't just referring to the church leaders. As Christians we all wear the rank of His ambassadors and have the right to exercise that authority.

In many ways our whole planet is a foreign court. Sin is at work here, contaminating everyone and everything. Once we become Christians, we have a sense in which earth is no longer our home. Paul reminds us in Ephesians that our citizenship is in heaven (see 2:19). But while we reside in this foreign court called Planet Earth, we are ambassadors for Christ. We didn't receive that rank of ambassador—the highest ranking official in a foreign court—by attending seminary or becoming a missionary. We received it when Jesus entered our lives, made us holy and fit for heaven and commissioned us to represent Him on earth.

Unleashing our churches and our potential for personal ministry means moving away from the world's fascination with titles and external credentials. The only title that really matters is the title of Christ-one. If you wear that title, you have authority as God's ambassador.

The longer I'm a believer, the more I see God's supply of material needs is often not dramatic. In fact, it is often like His supply of authority and time. In our affluent culture, He's often already supplied our needs; we just can't see it.

I don't mean to imply that the positions of pastor, elder or deacon are unimportant. They are intended by God for the good of the Church and should always be respected. So also should all the authority figures in other organizations and government be respected. But in order to respect these positions, Christians do not need to relinquish their own title as ambassadors for Christ.

As His ambassador, God can use you to introduce others to Jesus. You can lead a ministry, if God has gifted you and burdened your heart. You can do it because He has given you the authority to do it.

All the Materials We Need

Material needs are different from our needs for time and authority. Time and authority have already been entrusted to us. Not so with material resources.

Often God wants to use our need for material resources to teach us vital lessons about our dependence on Him. Dependence, however, is not intended to foster worry, but rather to develop faith. When Jesus taught His disciples in the Sermon on the Mount, He warned them of the pitfalls of worrying about material necessities. Instead He instructed them: "But first seek his kingdom and his righteousness, and all these things will be given to you as well" (Matt. 6:33).

God's Faithfulness. We can be confident that if we are seeking after God, He can and will supply all the necessary materials we need to do what work He has for us. But oftentimes we have no idea how He will supply.

Sometimes God supplies our material needs in dramatic ways. Like the time our church received a $50,000 gift at the beginning of our street ministry (see chap. 12).

Then there was the time when I was still in college, and my wife Mary and I wanted to invite some sailors over for Thanksgiving dinner. The only problem was we didn't have enough money to buy a turkey for our own family much less for three or four sailors. We simply decided to pray and ask God to provide us with enough money or food for our family plus the guests.

While we were praying, we heard a knock at the door. We opened it to find some people from the church we attended. They had brought us a turkey and enough food to feed a small navy! And since, we've seen God provide food, money, cars, and the list goes on.

I must confess in my early years as a Christian I was enamoured with God's dramatic provision of my needs and the needs of fellow Christians. But the longer I'm a believer, the more I see God's supply of material needs is often not dramatic. In fact, it is often like His supply of authority and time. In our affluent culture, He's often already supplied our needs; we just can't see it.

Such is the case a few years ago when some of the women in our church met to share their burden for crisis pregnancies. They wanted to establish a ministry, but all they could think of was how many resources they needed to run such a ministry. Their desire was to open a crisis pregnancy center, complete with a facility and staff. Of course that would have required a good-sized budget. It all seemed overwhelming.

So they decided to shift their thoughts. What if they tried to recruit couples in the church who had a spare bedroom to invite a woman in need to stay. Convinced they had hit upon a good idea, they began *Life Unlimited*.

Meanwhile in a neighboring state, an 18-year-old woman was about to leave her home and family and hitch-hike to Denver. Soon after arriving, Betty met a man who invited her to move in with him. She did, and things seemed to go OK, until one day she broke the news to him that she was pregnant.

That announcement did not turn out to be good news to her roommate; neither was the fact that she did not want an abortion. They began to have frequent fights and by her fourth month of pregnancy, he kicked her out.

While she was sitting out on the front lawn, Christian neighbors extended a helping hand. She told these Good Samaritans her story, which is a typical scenario behind the word *crisis* in a crisis pregnancy ministry. The couple knew about Life Unlimited, although they did not attend our church. They called to see if we could help.

Life Unlimited was able to place Betty in a shepherding home. Arnie and Valorie Snyder had an extra bedroom and a desire to serve the Lord. They became shepherds to Betty.

During her stay with the Snyders, Betty saw how a Christian husband treats his Christian wife. She attended church with them and eventually committed her life to Christ. Her baby Sara was born prematurely, and for the first time Betty had a support group in her life who really cared for her. They prayed, and Sara was soon able to leave the hospital. With Betty's permission we contacted her parents, who later came to Denver to take their daughter and new granddaughter back to their small town.

Shortly after she returned home, Betty wrote:

> Dear Pastor Frank,
>
> Thank you for all of the help that the people of Bear Valley Baptist Church gave to me. I really appreciate the financial help, and the home and family that Val and Arnie Snyder had given to me. Sara and I are doing fine; she now weighs 8 lbs. 2 oz. and is growing like a weed. There may be a possibility I will have a job this week. Thanks again, and I will write again later.
>
> Love,
Betty and Sara[2]

Over the past few years we have ministered to a couple hundred women in crisis pregnancy situations. The majority of the cases have been very successful. In some cases, there have been misunderstandings, but there is a risk in everything we do. The vast majority of women we have seen go through Life Unlimited have been helped, many of whom have found a personal relationship with Christ. And it has been accomplished for the most part with resources such as spare bedrooms, good marriages, a church family and the love of Christ. In other words, the materials to do the ministry had already been supplied.

Our faithfulness. So we see that God can and will supply any amount of materials we need, but first we need to be good stewards of the worldly wealth He has already entrusted us with. That worldly wealth may be a spare bedroom, as was the case with Arnie and Val Snyder. But often materials will, in one way or another, translate into money.

God taught me very early in my Christian life that He expected me to be faithful in the area of financial stewardship. Mary and I were involved in a Bible study when the question of tithing came up.

On the way home that evening, Mary asked me what I thought about giving 10 percent of our income to the Church. Now becoming a Christian hadn't changed the fact there never seemed to be enough money to buy the things we wanted and felt we needed, and I hadn't been a Christian long, but I knew how to dodge her question. I told her I'd pray about it.

A short time later, while I was in the army, I was given the opportunity to get a pay raise if I could pass a certain test. They called it proficiency pay. At the time I was making $270 per month, which, believe it or not, was enough to live quite well on, and if I passed this test I would get a $30 raise. I decided to make a deal with Mary and the Lord—a dangerous combination: If I passed the test I would give the $30 to the Lord's work.

When I sat down to take the test, I can remember the wave of disappointment that swept over me. The exam was to determine how well I understood my field, which was radar. But this test was on a system I had never seen before. Since it was a multiple-choice test, I had nothing to lose by guessing on nearly every question. After all, it was the Lord's money, if I passed. So I decided if He helped me guess right, fine; if not, it was His money we were losing.

I look back on that experience and wonder at my immaturity. I had been a Christian less than one year; one doesn't need to be very mature to realize that my deal with God was a form of gambling. I doubt that God enjoys playing the role of a holy slot machine. My only consolation when I reflect on this episode is that God knew He was dealing with a babe. He enabled me to guess well enough to score 61; passing was 60. The next year I failed the same test and lost the bonus pay. But that didn't matter, for by then I was committed to regular giving as part of my Christian life.

I'm not legalistic about tithing. But I do believe that more Christians sell out their ministry potential by not being faithful with money than for any other reason.

Jesus discussed what's at stake in the way we handle our money: "Whoever can be trusted with very little can also be trusted with much, and whoever is dishonest with very little will also be dishonest with much. So if you have not been trustworthy in handling worldly wealth, who will trust you with true riches?" (Luke 16:10-11).

To unleash our potential for God is impossible, if He can't trust us with true riches. Notice how Jesus contrasts worldly wealth with true riches. How we handle the former determines if God will give us the latter.

Unfortunately, amid our affluence we still have a vast number of Christians selling out just like the Old Testament Esau. Esau, we're told, sold his birthright for a "mess of pottage" (see Gen. 25). And when we fail to be faithful financial stewards, we sell out our potential for a mess of pottage.

God is able to supply our material needs to accomplish that which He has called us to. But first we need to ask: What resources do we already have? and, Are we being good stewards of the resources God has already given us?

THE KING HAS GIVEN US PERMISSION

I believe this is a day for both individual Christians and local churches to be brimming with godly confidence. In America we live in a culture that can easily be penetrated by the gospel. That's also true in many other countries in the free world.

A letter I received recently from Australia is a case in point. Just over a year prior to receiving this letter, I had traveled "down under" to spend some extended time with a church in the suburbs of Sydney. Since then the pastor of that church, Paul de Plater, and I continue to correspond. His most recent letter shared much encouraging news:

> At the present time, the Unleashed Ministries are really getting underway in our church and we are rather excited so far in what we are seeing. These include at the moment a wilderness experience for kids of low self-esteem. It also includes a special educational training for those who are below the normal educational standards, ministering not only to the children but to their families; also a ministry to aged care people in one of our local hospitals, and we are seeing each of these has great fruit for ministry.
> In the pipeline for the coming year we see a

number of ministries emerging. Among these is a special ministry to unemployed, another for young people facing drug and alcohol problems at school, a special drug education programme in schools which is now underway successfully. A young girl graduating from college this year is keen to use her social work degree in commencing a ministry to girls who are pregnant and at risk.

We have already set up and started to care for youth at risk, and this is successful thus far and we thank the Lord for that. We have already commenced a grandmothers' ministry in the life of the church and this is a special ministry to young mothers and in actual fact is the reverse tangent of the MOPS programme.[3]

As I reflected on Pastor Paul's words, I couldn't help but think back on my time with him and his church. Though I tried to encourage them and share some things we learned about the ministry-oriented church here in Denver, I can't say that I had a lot to offer these folks. They were already a healthy, progressive, growing and ministry-oriented church. Yet it sounded as if they had had an unusual year of outreach since my last visit.

It occurred to me finally that perhaps the most important thing I had done was to give them *permission* to have an attitude toward ministry possibilities that says the sky's the limit!

One of the things Nehemiah did for the people of Jerusalem was to bring them permission from King Artaxerxes to rebuild the wall. One of the reasons the people of Judah lived so long amid the rubble was fear that the king of Persia would crush any attempt to rebuild their wall. Nehemiah, on the other hand, assures them that the king says it's OK!

Let me assure you today, the King says it's OK to unleash the potential for ministry He has given to every believer!

EXPLORING YOUR POTENTIAL

1. Nehemiah was a slave with no resources for the job he felt called to do. God provided for Nehemiah just as He promises to do for you. What are the three resources listed in this chapter for unleashing your God-given potential for ministry?

2. Do you feel you are a good manager of time? Is there room for improvement? If so, what steps could you take to be a better steward of the time God has given you?

3. What title gives us the authority to unleash our God-given potential for ministry?

4. Could your church institute a ministry like Life Unlimited? What resources do you and your church members

already have to carry on such a ministry?

5. On a scale of 1-10 (10 being high) rate yourself as to your financial stewardship. Be honest with yourself. Could God trust you with real (ministry) riches because you've been financially faithful?

1	2	3	4	5	6	7	8	9	10

Not
very
faithful

Very
faithful

Notes
1. Reprinted from *Engineering Management Society Newsletter,* November-December 1982.
2. The names of the signatories have been changed to protect their privacy.
3. The Reverend Paul de Plater in a personal letter to the author. Used by permission.

CHAPTER 7

Why We Don't See the Ruins

She invited me in and asked me to be seated at the kitchen table. It was a modest apartment, though I doubt Rosemary saw it that way. It was probably the nicest place she had ever lived.

Rosemary was a street kid who began attending our church as a result of Genesis Center, a communal home we ran in the early days of our street ministry. While Rosemary was living at the Genesis Center she met Jim. Eventually they married and managed to move into their own little apartment.

Now Rosemary wanted to be baptized. And since I planned to do the baptizing I had stopped by to talk to her about how she had become a Christian. Like most of the people we meet in the streets, Rosemary's story was incredibly painful.

She related how, by the time she was 15, she had had

a baby. One day she was sitting with her boyfriend—not the baby's father—in his parked car. They got into an argument and the boyfriend threw the baby out the window, then drove off.

The authorities took the baby away from Rosemary, the boyfriend split and Rosemary was alone. She hitchhiked to Denver and our street ministry workers met her shortly after she arrived.

Unfortunately, Rosemary's story is all too common. Over the past 15 years of pastoring, I have heard countless versions of the same story. To grasp the magnitude of ruined lives in our culture is impossible.

Not long ago, Youth for Christ issued the following statistics:

> Every 24 hours in the U.S.—
> 13,700 kids become victims of broken homes
> 5,400 run away
> 32,876 take some form of narcotic
> 1,370 attempt suicide
> 3,287 become pregnant
> 1,389 have an abortion
> 10,958 are beaten, molested or abused. [1]

That our society is producing enormous amounts of human ruin all around us is obvious. We constantly hear alarming statistics on divorce, drug addiction and overpopulation in our jails. But statistics tend to bounce off us, and we eventually become immune to their impact.

While numbers may be impersonal, people are not. When the cold statistics become people, the impact of their plight carries a big punch.

Jack is another story. He wrote me recently: "Look at me, you took me from the streets, placed me in a home with real values and love, and helped me straighten my mixed values and morals."

When Jack was 14 his parents divorced. Neither of them wanted Jack to live with them. So, not knowing what else to do, he hitchhiked from his home in Miami to San Francisco to live with his brother.

When Jack's brother came home one night, Jack was waiting outside his apartment.

"What are you doing here, man?" his brother asked.

"I've come to live with you," Jack replied.

"No, you haven't!" his brother said, as he walked passed Jack into his apartment, closing the door behind him.

Jack was now on his own. Again, not knowing what else to do, he came to Denver in search of a "Rocky Mountain High." Our street workers met him near the state capitol at a notorious hangout for homosexuals. Young male prostitutes mean big money for their pimps. Fortunately, Jack had not gotten involved, but on the street the name of the game is survival, and things like prostitution are just a matter of time for people like Jack.

Jack accepted an invitation to stay at the Genesis Center and, while living there he committed his life to Christ. Eventually he moved in with one of our church families. He later graduated from high school and joined the military.

Not all of Jack's problems have been solved. But when the statistics are figured, he can be included among those who are genuine believers in Jesus Christ, members of a church, high school graduates. Hopefully, he also will receive an honorable discharge from the military.

Those aren't exactly accomplishments to list in anyone's WHO'S WHO, but they are a lot better than, say, drug addict, prostitute and jail inmate.

The stories of the Rosemarys and Jacks raise a critical question for the contemporary followers of Jesus. Simply put, we must ask, Why are we so out of touch with people who represent the ruins of our culture? It doesn't take a Rhodes scholar to figure out that if our churches are out of touch with these people, the individual Christians in our churches are also out of touch.

But why are we so out of touch? Four possible explanations come immediately to mind:

1. Too many of us Christians are culturally and geographically removed from those who represent the ruins of our society.
2. Too many of us adhere to a half-loaf gospel.
3. We overlook the abuse of wealth and power.
4. We hoard our resources.

Let's take a closer look at each of these hindrances to our seeing what both Nehemiah and Jesus saw.

We Are Too Far from the Ruins

Ruins are generally depressing. Of course, such ruins as we find in Athens or Rome are admirable. But ruined people, like the ruined wall of Jerusalem in Nehemiah's day, are not a cause for rejoicing. On the contrary, when Nehemiah heard that the walls lay in rubble, he wept (see Neh. 1:4).

Living in beautiful, distant Susa, Nehemiah had been out of touch with the ruins surrounding Jerusalem. In fact, because he spent most of his time in the royal palace, he probably knew little about even the slums of Susa itself.

The tragedy and disgrace of the broken walls had not been among his immediate concerns.

Fortunately for God's people in Jerusalem, he didn't try to avoid coming into direct contact with the ruins. Instead, when he arrived in Jerusalem, before he ever challenged the people to rebuild the wall, he took an extensive trip around the city to view the rubble.

The scene is somber as Nehemiah sets out at night to see the shambles of the city. He decided to tour the ruined wall by the light of the moon when nothing could break his concentration; he wanted to feel the full impact. Consequently, he developed a heart that beat with God's heart, enabling him to see beyond his own needs and circumstances to the needs of others. He was able to see through the eyes of Jesus.

Seeing the Needs of Others

I wonder what would happen if we, like Nehemiah, would go for a walk down the streets of our cities by the light of the moon. At least in Nehemiah's case, the ruins he viewed were of bricks; for us, they would be people like Rosemary and Jack.

Our neighborhoods and offices are not places where we make contact with the Rosemarys and Jacks. And, sad to say, neither are our churches, for we worship in middle-class fortresses from which we cannot even see the spiritual and cultural ruins of our society. That we remain so distant from the human ruins in our culture is a continuing tragedy.

A few years ago, a couple living in the Genesis Center decided to witness in various gay bars in our city. I told our congregation that we now had a witness in the homosexual bars. Several people came up to me later and told me they didn't know such a thing as homosexual bars even existed.

I once sat down with a man who is a recognized leader of church renewal in America. The churches that have begun under his influence are generally white middle-class churches. When I began to talk about ministries to street people, to people in jails, to unwed mothers and so on, he admitted such ministries were foreign to the churches he was associated with. In those churches, the biggie in ministries is home Bible study. But it's awfully hard to see the ruins of our cities when we drive only from one middle-class neighborhood to another for yet another session of Bible study.

Most of us live in our middle-class suburbs. We wake up in the morning to the sound of soft music. We shower, put on our deodorant and drive to our offices in our comfortable cars.

While we're on the road, we turn on more soft music and, if it's warm, the air-conditioning as well. In our offices, we rub shoulders with others who are well-scrubbed and sweet-smelling. There we enjoy background music and more air-conditioning. It's all so nice.

From such lofty heights, how can we ever see someone like Rosemary? And if *we* don't see her, who will? Rosemary needs some of the resources we have, like a place to stay or healthy models of husband-wife relationships. Of course, what she needs most of all is for someone to tell her about Jesus.

But she has something to offer us as well. Street people tend to be much more people-oriented than thing-oriented. For them, life is not a matter of voracious consumption filled with concern over portfolios, house payments, getting the latest computer or designer clothes. Rather their concerns are centered around one objective: the struggle to survive.

At Bear Valley we have found that exposure to street people is often a challenge both to our middle-class materialism and to our timidity in sharing the gospel. And when a street person does come to Christ, his or her childlike

---

Perhaps we should enforce a new rule in our churches that says, for every hour we spend in a worship service, Sunday School class, Bible study, discipleship group or social fellowship, we must spend an equal amount of time in direct ministry, meeting the needs of someone else.

---

faith and boldness in sharing that faith can be a great encouragement to the rest of the Body.

Meeting the Needs of Others

A couple of years ago, our church opened a medical clinic in one of the poorest areas of our city. We'll talk about the clinic more later, but for now let me simply point out that most of the people in our church have always had their own private doctors and dentists.

We middle-class Americans usually take good medical care for granted. But many of the people who live where we opened our clinic have never had their own private doctor or dentist. For them, medicine had always been an impersonal social-service-type experience. Now, some of them have their own private doctors and dentists, just like most people in my part of town. They have this personalized health care because some Christian people see others the way Jesus saw them. Jesus not only saw them as individuals, He saw their needs as well.

Recently, one cold snowy winter evening, Mary and I

had settled in for a comfortable evening at home with a fire in the fireplace and a video on the life of the Russian dissenter, Andrey Sakharov. But before we had a chance to finish dinner, the phone rang. At the other end of the line was a distressed female voice. She explained that she and her husband desperately needed gas, food and shelter for the evening. She had called another church, and they gave her our number.

A couple of hours later, as I drove home from the motel, I put them in for the evening, I reflected on the words of Paul in Philippians 2:4, "Each of you should look not only to your own interests, but also to the interests of others." And I thought how different my interests were that evening from those of that couple.

I had been interested only in getting a fire built and hoping that the Sakharov video was in good working order. But the couple who had just entered my life had concerns of a totally different nature. They were concerned about where their next meal was coming from, a warm place to stay and gas for their car's empty tank. And those were just their immediate needs. Because those same concerns had already been met in my own life, it was difficult for me to empathize with people in their situation.

Perhaps we should enforce a new rule in our churches that says, for every hour we spend in a worship service, Sunday School class, Bible study, discipleship group or social fellowship, we must spend an equal amount of time in direct ministry, meeting the needs of someone else.

A growing number of evangelicals believe that something less than a full-loaf gospel emerged from the infamous Liberal-Fundamentalist Controversy that erupted in the late nineteenth century. In his book *Megatruth,* David McKenna points out, "For some reason, in the split of the Church between liberal and conservative factions, the concerns for social justice tended to go with the liberals while conservatives continued to be identified with acts of personal mercy."[2]

One of the results of this conflict was that each side came away with a half-loaf gospel. Liberals preach a gospel of saving humankind by social action. Since, in their theology, hell is a mythical place, the real good news is that

---

Both the Old and New Testaments make it clear that the biblical gospel is full-loaf. The gospel is good news for both *the body and the soul; good news for the* whole *person, for all this life and the life yet to come.*

---

someone will help you become better off today right here on Planet Earth.

Fundamentalists, on the other hand, contend that hell is a real place and all that matters is the destiny of a man's soul in eternity. Social action, they felt, was a ploy of the devil to sidetrack us from proclaiming the *real* gospel. Christians under this influence were not encouraged, but rather discouraged from mixing with the world, no matter the circumstance or reason.

Both the Old and New Testaments make it clear that the biblical gospel is full-loaf. The gospel is good news for *both* the body and the soul; good news for the *whole* person, for all this life and the life yet to come. In the Old Testament, for example, God's concern for the poor is a major theme (see Exod. 23:11; Deut. 15:7; Ps. 35:10; Prov. 19:17; Jer. 20:13.).

Concern for the poor is also clearly an issue for Jesus. He described what Judgment Day will be like when He told His disciples:

"Then the King will say to those on his right,
'Come, you who are blessed by my Father; take
your inheritance, the kingdom prepared for you
since the creation of the world. For I was hungry and you gave me something to eat, I was
thirsty and you gave me something to drink, I
was a stranger and you invited me in, I needed
clothes and you clothed me, I was sick and you
looked after me, I was in prison and you came
to visit me' . . . The King will reply, 'I tell you
the truth, whatever you did for one of the least
of these brothers of mine, you did for me'"
(Matt. 25:34-36,40).

Note that this passage hasn't one word about explain-
ing a plan of salvation. Nor is there any hint in the parable
of the Good Samaritan that he verbalized the "Four Spiritual Laws" as he helped the merchant who had been
beaten and robbed (see Luke 10:25-37).

On the other hand, our Lord was clear with Nicodemus
that to see the Kingdom of God, one must be born again
(see John 3:3). When the people asked the apostles what
they should do to be saved, Peter didn't reply, "Go, help
the poor"; he said, "Repent, and be baptized every one of
you, in the name of Jesus Christ for the remission of your
sins" (Acts 2:38, *KJV*).

The Biblical Gospel Is Balanced

There is throughout Scripture a balanced message of the
whole gospel for the whole person. As followers of Jesus,
we must be concerned about both a person's social welfare
and their soul. In *Unleashing the Church,* I discuss the

problem Jesus faced because His disciples very often did not see what He saw. In Samaria, for example, He had to tell them, "Open your eyes and look at the fields! They are ripe for harvest" (John 4:35).

A major challenge in the venture of unleashing our potential is learning to see through the eyes of Jesus. Our Lord was able to see tax collectors and Samaritan women. He saw people that the average Jew of His day couldn't see. But more, He saw their needs.

Therefore, when the apostle Paul challenges the believers in Philippi to have a mind like Jesus, he tells them: "Each of you should look not only to your own interests, but also to the interests of others" (Phil. 2:4).

Paul assumes we will see and be committed to our own interests, and that's OK. But he also pleads with us to see beyond our own interests, something that probably won't come naturally. In fact, I think it's fair to say he assumed even believers were not likely to be naturally committed to the needs of others. We need to ask: If Jesus were on earth today would He be committed to touching the lives of those who are in ruins? Of course, He would! We know that's the right answer based on His time on earth 2,000 years ago, when He consistently sought out the human ruins and ministered to them.

Well, Jesus is on Planet Earth today! He's living in the hearts of all who have confessed Him as Lord and Savior. And one of His primary missions is to enable us to see people ruined by sin, to see people through His eyes. That is why He said that we are to be salt and light (see Matt. 5:13-14); yet, many of our churches are saying, "Stay away from a corrupt and dying world!"

Jesus saw the whole person, and if we are going to see people through the eyes of Jesus, we have to look after both their spiritual needs and their physical needs.

Meanwhile, until our churches catch sight of the ruined lives around us and accept responsibility for rebuilding these lives in Christ, it seems that those who are reaching out to the Rosemarys and Jacks of our society will continue doing their ministries independently. I have been encouraged as I travel across the states to find believers who, on their own, have opened their homes and/or visited jails, even though they may receive little or no encouragement from their churches. These people, however, are rare.

We Overlook the Abuse of Wealth and Power

At first glance, chapter 5 of Nehemiah doesn't quite make sense. Up to this point, Nehemiah has relentlessly pursued the rebuilding of the wall. He has wept, fasted, mourned, risked his life, traveled a great distance, motivated people, withstood pressure from without and overcome discouragement from within. In other words, nothing has stopped this man from pursuing the rebuilding of the wall.

Yet in chapter 5, only a single mention is made of the work on the wall. It's almost as though Nehemiah says, "Forget the wall, I've lost interest in trying to rebuild it." What possibly could have triggered this dramatic change?

This dramatic change in Nehemiah is brought about when he becomes aware that some of the people of Jerusalem are exploiting the poor. At this point, Nehemiah's number one objective is to stop the exploitation, not just to finish the wall.

A pressing question for every generation of God's people is simply, If God gives us wealth and power, will we use it for ourselves or will we use it to help the poor and powerless? Nehemiah 5:14-16 answers that question as far as Nehemiah is concerned:

> Moreover, from the twentieth year of King Artaxerxes, when I was appointed to be their governor in the land of Judah, until his thirty-second year—twelve years—neither I nor my brothers ate the food allotted to the governor. But the earlier governors—those preceding me—placed a heavy burden on the people and took forty shekels of silver from them in addition to food and wine. Their assistants also lorded it over the people. *But out of reverence for God I did not act like that.* Instead, I devoted myself to the work on this wall. All my men were assembled there for the work; *we did not acquire any land* (emphasis mine).

As Christians, we need to be asking ourselves, Are we hoarding our ministry potential? We need to consider our resources.

Can we read? If so, we might tutor someone who is having reading problems. Recent studies have revealed that one out of eight adults in America is illiterate.

Can we speak English? Then we might lead conversational English classes for international students, refugees, migrants and so on.

If the white Christian community in America is the most resource-laden that has ever existed, we individually need to be asking, How can I use my resources?

Investing Our Resources

My nephew Tom Tillapaugh and his wife Yvonne have pondered that question about their resources. Tom has a master's degree in education; Yvonne is a licensed practical nurse. Those credentials represent a lot of power. But instead of marketing those degrees for all they can get, they have come to Denver to open the Denver Street School in conjunction with Andy Cannon's street ministry.

While running a communal home for street people Tom and Yvonne are working with school drop-outs as well. The street school recently had its first graduation. Among the three graduates was Sharon.

We will never reach our ministry potential when we consume our resources on ourselves. For us to realize our potential, we must give ourselves to the needs of others rather than endlessly pursuing more for ourselves.

If you were to meet Sharon today, you would never guess she lived through four years of personal hell. Even though she was raised in a Christian home, she dropped out of school and got married when she was 18. She and her husband got involved in a cult, heavy-metal rock music and were hooked on drugs.

As their intake of speed (methamphetamine) increased, Sharon's husband began to get stronger and stronger anti-God messages from the rock music. One day after staying high and going without sleep for five days, he "cast out God, and the demons came in." As Sharon tells it, "He looked like he was already in hell."

Sharon, her husband and their daughter moved around

a lot. Eventually they moved to Denver and were staying in a downtown shelter, when Sharon took their child and left her husband. She started frequenting our Jesus on Main Street Coffee House (JOMS). At JOMS, Sharon says she met people who were "honest, open and comfortable."

It was at JOMS that Tom Tillapaugh introduced himself to Sharon and offered her the possibility of earning her high school diploma. She was hesitant, but finally agreed to take the entrance tests. In September 1986, she started going to the Denver Street School and, in February 1987, she and her 3-year-old daughter moved into Tom and Yvonne's discipleship home. "They helped me so much with my self-esteem and helped me to think I'm worthwhile. The school got my brain working logically again, instead of all the craziness of what speed did to me. Tom helped me do my tax forms for the last five years. He cares about me for who I am. They even trust me with their kids and really make me want to make it. Yvonne's a great cook and I've gone from 98 pounds to 120. And now I'm graduating!"

Sharon is so proud of her graduation and of her beautiful graduation ring that has her birthstone, name and the insignia "A New Beginning." She strongly believes God has protected her through four terrible years. Now at 22, she has lived a lifetime. Her daughter is doing well, and Sharon is so thankful to still have her. Regarding her future, she may move back in with her parents or continue on for more schooling.

Sharon concludes, "My life is good now. I don't deserve such blessings from God. I want to get stabilized in my life and eventually be able to help other hurting women who are going through what I went through."

Giving Ourselves

In today's world are scores of Sharons. I wonder what Nehemiah would do if he were here to see us building great supermarket-type churches, schools and para organizations to service an over-indulged middle class, amid so much human ruin.

And the sad part is that we will never reach our ministry potential when we consume our resources on ourselves. For us to realize our potential, we must give ourselves to the needs of others rather than endlessly pursuing more for ourselves.

If we want to live, we must die. That's one of the many paradoxes Jesus taught (see John 12:24-25). If we really want to get what God has for us we must give—give of our resources and ourselves. We must give a gospel message that's clear concerning the issues of salvation. After all what does it profit anyone to gain the world and lose his soul (see Luke 9:25)?

We dare not make the same mistake as the liberals who only minister to people's social needs. But we also dare not stop with a verbal message of salvation. We must learn to communicate the whole of God's gospel, the good news, to the whole person's needs.

We're not likely to be very committed to the giving of our resources or ourselves, unless we're convinced that God's call for our lives is genuinely significant, and we are able to see the ruined people of this world through the eyes of Jesus.

EXPLORING YOUR POTENTIAL

1. Is your life-style such that you come in contact with the Jacks and Rosemarys of this world? If not, what adjust-

ments could you make in your daily routine to get in touch with this part of our population?

2. Although our neighborhoods and offices are generally not in the areas where the Jacks and Rosemarys are found, serious human needs exist in those places too. What kinds of needs do you see in (a) your workplace, (b) your neighborhood, (c) your community?

3. What are some of the steps you could take to develop the kind of "eyesight" Jesus displayed? Are you willing to move out of your comfort zone from time to time to see the needs of others?

4. What is the difference between the full-loaf and the half-loaf gospel? Looking back, what line of thinking dominates the churches you have been a part of? Do you adhere to a full-loaf or half-loaf gospel?

Notes
1. Extracted from the personal support letter of a Youth for Christ staffer.
2. David McKenna, *Megatruth* (San Bernardino, CA: Here's Life, Publishers, 1987), p. 123.

CHAPTER 8

The Society of Gamblers for God

Are you a risk-taker? Probably not. Most of us quite naturally pull back from risk. We actually like the idea of risk, but we'd rather experience it vicariously. So we pay to watch others take chances and buy tickets to watch the flying trapeze act at the circus. Or we turn on the TV, sit back in our recliner chairs and watch cliff divers at Acapulco.

Risk-takers are often entertainers for the rest of us. For most people, life is primarily concerned with creating safety and predictability. One of the greatest human pursuits is the pursuit of comfort zones.

The problem with pursuing safety and predictability, however, is that the result is often terribly boring. In his book, *Risking*, David Viscott reminds us that if we never risked, we would never move away from home, find a job, ask for a raise, make a friend, fall in love.[1]

Some time ago, while leading a worship in Kansas City,

I had an unusual—and, in hindsight, humorous—occasion to reflect on Viscott's list of risk. The workshop I led was packed with about 200 people, perhaps 20 of whom were women. Two of those 20 were sitting in the front row, which was fine with me. Fine, that is, until one of the men held up a note for me to read that said, "Your zipper is open!" and I was speaking without a podium!

At that moment I could have shot those women for being in the front row. But as I thought about Viscott's list, I realized that if I hadn't risked getting up in front of that group in the first place, I wouldn't have faced this dilemma. Risk is the spice of life, but there are always moments when we wish life were a little more bland.

The accounts abound in Scriptures of men and women who were risk-takers. They range from the famous such as Abraham, to the obscure Epaphroditus.

About Abraham we are told: "By faith Abraham, when called to go to a place he would later receive as his inheritance, obeyed and went, even though he did not know where he was going" (Heb. 11:8). One item the writer of Hebrews didn't mention was that Abraham was 75 years old when he set out for the Promised Land.

The little-known Epaphroditus was a messenger to the apostle Paul from the church at Philippi. He was sent by the Philippian church to Rome to help the imprisoned Paul. When Paul got ready to send him back, he instructed the Philippian believers to: "Welcome him in the Lord with great joy, and honor men like him, because he almost died for the work of Christ, risking his life to make up for the help you could not give me" (Phil. 2:29-30).

The phrase Paul uses to say Epaphroditus risked his life is a Greek idiom that literally means, "He staked his life on a throw of the dice." Epaphroditus was a gambler for God.

Christians have three good reasons why they ought to be champions of risk, a society of gamblers for God:

1. We have nothing to lose.
2. We have freedom to fail.
3. We have faith to face discomfort and fear.

Few of us are asked to risk our lives, but all of us are asked to risk such things as friends, reputation, job and security when we follow Jesus Christ. Yet, whatever the risk, the truth remains that we have nothing to lose that is more important than being obedient to our Lord.

NOTHING TO LOSE

One of the great truths in the believer's identification with Christ is simply that we really have nothing to lose. Paul declared to the Galatians "I have been crucified with Christ and I no longer live, but Christ lives in me" (Gal. 2:20). He also told the Philippians only one thing mattered—that "Christ will be exalted in my body, whether by life or by death" (Phil. 1:20). Then immediately in the next verse, he captures the reason believers are free to be risk-takers: "For to me, to live is Christ and to die is gain" (1:21).

We have nothing to lose; death for Christians is victory. That truth enabled Jim Elliot and four other missionaries, all martyred by the Auca Indians in Ecuador, to risk their lives. Elliot wrote in his diary, "He is no fool who gives what he knows he cannot keep, to gain what he knows he cannot lose."[2]

We are free. Jesus said that if He would make us free we would be free indeed (see John 8:36). Whenever the challenge to risk arises, we might ask ourselves, What would be the worst possible thing that could happen if I take this risk? At times we might trace our line of reasoning back to, "I could lose my life." That's certainly one of the most dramatic possibilities, but even then we are winners. We have nothing to lose, not even life.

Epaphroditus risked his life, as did the apostle Paul and Jim Elliot. But God seldom asks His followers to risk their lives as these men did. Most of us tend to face risks more like the one Denny and Mary Axtell faced shortly after they became Christians.

The Axtells had become Christians at an evangelistic dinner party. They later told me about their anxiety as they arrived for this "religious event." Actually, they were scared to death. They sat in their car and debated about going in. They reasoned, "If we can just make it to the bar for some predinner drinks, we will be all right." Later, they related to me their keen disappointment when they found out the predinner drinks were nonalcoholic. A couple of shots of courage would certainly have helped, they felt.

Once inside, however, their uneasiness gave way to a feeling of identification with the speaker. Adolph Coors IV of the famous brewery family related how he and his wife had both committed their lives to Christ. He went on to tell how their marriage had been healed and how life had become meaningful for them now that they were living for the Lord.

Mary and Denny identified with some of the struggles Adolph Coors had shared. They also identified with his struggle to turn his life over to Christ. And just as they had found the courage to get out of their car and come in to

the dinner, they also found courage to say yes to Christ
and to invite Him into their lives.

About a year after they made their commitment to follow Jesus, our church sponsored another evangelistic dinner. Denny and Mary decided to risk inviting several of
their non-Christian friends. I can remember Mary
approaching me in the foyer of the church with a concerned look on her face. She told me, "Frank, we've
invited most of our non-Christian friends to attend the dinner; I'm afraid this could cost us their friendships." Then
after she thought about what she had just said, she added,
"Oh well, I guess we'll just leave that part of it with the
Lord; if we lose the friendships, we lose them."

Yes, few of us are asked to risk our lives, but all of us
are asked to risk such things as friends, reputation, job
and security when we follow Jesus Christ. Yet, whatever
the risk, the truth remains that we have nothing to lose
that is more important than being obedient to our Lord. I
once heard a speaker refer to evangelicals as "evan-
jellyfish." His point being, we often don't have the courage
to risk because we're too afraid of what we might lose.

Freedom to risk, however, is not limited to those who
have enough courage to risk their lives or even the scorn
of their friends. Freedom to risk is for all of us who know
Jesus. As the apostle Paul puts it, "If God is for us, who
can be against us?" (Rom. 8:31).

Because of Christ, you are free to risk. Remember,
you won't have to take that risk in your own strength. As a
child of God, you have the privilege of risking in the light of
His sovereign strength.

FREEDOM TO FAIL

Another reason Christians are free to risk is because it's

OK for us to fail. God is not primarily interested in success, rather He is interested in faithfulness and effort.

Earlier I referred to Epaphroditus, the man the apostle Paul wrote about in Philippians. Epaphroditus was a risk-taker. Yet, interestingly, Epaphroditus's mission, in the eyes of Paul, was not a raving success. He had come to Rome to serve Paul, but instead became ill, homesick and distressed that his loved ones in Philippi were worried about him. This turn of events caused Paul to have anxiety over the situation. So instead of being a help to Paul, Epaphroditus was actually a burden.

Paul decided to send Epaphroditus back to his people. Yet look what Paul has to say about this man:

> But I think it is necessary to send back to you Epaphroditus, my brother, fellow worker and fellow soldier, who is also your messenger, whom you sent to take care of my needs . . . . Welcome him in the Lord with great joy, and honor men like him, because he almost died for the work of Christ, risking his life to make up for the help you could not give me. (Phil. 2:25,29-30).

Paul makes it sound like Epaphroditus's ministry had been a genuine success. We know differently. Yet Paul saw something that was far more important than success. He saw a man of obedience and faithfulness. God asks nothing more of you or me.

Several years ago, we decided to try a Saturday evening service at our church. Rather than split families up for the Sunday School hour, we decided to conduct an intergenerational-type class and keep the family units together. Barbara Linville, a professional writer in our church, volunteered to write the curriculum; she invested dozens of hours into the project. We had some great services and some good family class sessions.

This approach had a dynamic that we all liked very much. Parents and children worked on projects that helped them interact on the main point of the Bible passage we were studying that week. But in the end the whole Saturday night worship and family Sunday School experiment did not work out as we had hoped it would. You might say that idea failed. But that didn't diminish the faithfulness of Barbara and everyone involved in this risky venture.

Because we are free to fail, we are free to risk. Some of the world's greatest successes failed far more often than they ever succeeded. Look at this illustration from the like of Abraham Lincoln:

> "Perhaps one of the most dramatic examples in history of perseverance in the face of repeated defeat is in the professional record of Abraham Lincoln.
> He lost his job in 1832.
> He was defeated for the legislature, also in 1832.
> He failed in business in 1833.
> He was elected to the legislature in 1843.
> He suffered the loss of his sweetheart, who died in 1835.
> He suffered a nervous breakdown in 1836.
> He was defeated for speaker of the state legislature in 1838.
> He was defeated for nomination for Congress in 1843.
> He was elected to Congress in 1846.

He lost his renomination for Congress in 1848.
He was rejected for the position of land officer in 1849.
He was defeated for the Senate in 1854.
He was defeated for the nomination for Vice President of the United States in 1856.
He was defeated again for Senate in 1858.
Abraham Lincoln was elected President of the United States in 1860.[3]

Risk forces us away from ourselves and demands that we depend upon our Lord. And our dependence upon Him enables us to serve Him outside our normal comfort zones.

FAITH TO FACE DISCOMFORT AND FEAR

In chapter 2 of Nehemiah, our hero faced an agonizing situation. In verse 2 he tells us, "I was very much afraid." He had good reason to be; to enter the presence of the king with a sad face—unless a person was physically ill—was a capital crime. Nehemiah was not ill, but he decided that it was time to let the king see how he really felt.

The moment was tense. Nehemiah faced an agonizing situation: Either he remained in his world of secluded weeping and mourning, or he had to put his life on the line. This situation is clearly one that faced him outside his comfort zone.

Perhaps the ultimate example of someone being forced outside his comfort zone is Jesus struggling before the

Father in the Garden of Gethsemane. He faced the cross. And one thing certain about a cross, it has no comfort zones.

Yes, the cross is the ultimate illustration that risk forces us out of our comfort zones. And God does call some of His followers to specific times of risking in their lives. But for most of us, our struggles will not be as dramatic as was that of Nehemiah before the king or that of Jesus sweating blood in the Garden of Gethsemane. Our struggles are more likely to be like those of a young preschool mother by the name of Denise Wister.

When Denise and her family moved to Denver, she was invited to attend a Mothers of Preschoolers (MOPS) meeting at our church. The atmosphere of MOPS was supportive and nonthreatening to Denise. It was just what she needed during her time of transition to a new city.

Although Denise was a Christian, she had not grown much spiritually. But before long both Denise and her husband Dennis attended worship services, where Dennis committed his life to Christ. Shortly after, they were both baptized.

Denise then began to reach out to other preschool moms by inviting them to MOPS. She was learning the important element of risk by allowing herself to be stretched.

She said to me: "By nature, I am not an extrovert and taking any leadership was a definite test of faith for me. Through MOPS leadership I learned that in order to grow, I had to step out in faith and not use my excuses, but rely on the Lord. I eventually [a process of six years] became the coordinator for Tuesday MOPS at Bear Valley for 40 women and 90 children. There's no way you could have told me five years earlier that I could have done this."

R.C. Sproul of Liganier Ministries says he is fond of

asking his students a trick question. He inquires, "Which of God's prohibitions do you suppose occurs most frequently in Scripture?"

Students, according to Sproul, immediately think of "thou shalt not lie, steal, murder and so on." But remember this is a trick question. The answer is not any of the "thou shalt nots"; rather it is "fear not." Yes, of all the negative commands of Scripture, "fear not" is the one repeated most often.

Well, Nehemiah did fear. But God saw him through. After all, the worst that could have happened was that he lost his life. Yet even if he had, he was still a winner because his God is Lord over death.

Nehemiah could possibly have failed in his attempt to get the wall rebuilt. But we know that success is not the issue. What is important is that in his attempt, Nehemiah was faithful to his Lord.

Nehemiah is where we need to be from time to time, out of our comfort zones. And when we are, if God has led us there, we can relax, because over and over again we're encouraged by God's Word to "fear not."

Again, Christians are free to risk, because (1) we have nothing to lose, (2) it's okay to fail and (3) faith equips us to handle discomfort and fear. Risk forces us away from ourselves and demands that we depend upon our Lord. And our dependence upon Him enables us to serve Him outside our normal comfort zones.

Unleashing our God-given potential will require risk. But, like Abraham, Nehemiah and Epaphroditus, we are official members of the Society of Gamblers for God.

EXPLORING YOUR POTENTIAL

1. Can you think of a situation or dilemma you found your-

self in at one time or another because you ventured to take a risk? What was the outcome?

2. How would you compare the faith exhibited by Abraham, Nehemiah and Epaphroditus? How does your faith in times of risk compare with that of these Bible personalities?

3. List the three reasons why Christians should be champions of risk. Relate each of these three reasons to the ministry potential you see for yourself, your church.

4. The words "fear not" appear through the Old and New Testaments. Using a concordance, familiarize yourself with some of the relevant Scripture verses. What is God's provision for you to fear not. Relate this truth to your own potential for ministry.

Notes
1. David Viscott, *Risking* (New York: Simon & Schuster, Inc.: Pocket Books, Inc., 1983).
2. Jim Elliot, *The Journal of Jim Elliot* (Old Tappan, NJ: Fleming H. Revell Co., 1978).
3. Source unknown.

PART THREE
Unleashing Your Potential

CHAPTER 9

Your Special Call to Ministry

When Christ comes into our lives and identifies us with Himself, He brings with Him a general call to the Christian life and to the ministry. In other words, no matter what our profession or position in life, if Christ has taken up residency in our lives, we are called to have a witness and to minister to the needs of one another.

Much of life's ministry is not sought out; it's given to us in our families and in our occupations—in other words, in our general living. And to be effective witnesses, servants and disciples in our Christian lives, even without any special call to ministry, every believer must make certain basic, personal commitments to:

1. A daily devotional time,
2. The study of God's Word,

3. A consistent and serious prayer life,
4. A personal commitment to the Great Commission,
5. A life-style that is totally pleasing to God.

DISCERNING YOUR CALL TO A SPECIAL MINISTRY?

True, lay people generally don't think of their ministry calling beyond that which arises in their daily living. Popularly, pastors, missionaries, gospel musicians and others in what is often described as "full-time Christian service" are those who are thought to receive special calls to ministry, but not so the average Joe Pewsitter.

Yet I believe God has more than a general call for every believer; He also has a special call for each of us, even though we do not always discern it. You are already serving Him in a general way in your family and occupation. But you sense He is calling you to more. And you are not quite sure what that special call might be.

So how do we discern God's special call?

Philippians 2:13 is a key verse in helping us understand how God works. "For it is God who is at work within you, giving you the will and the power to achieve his purpose" (Phillips).

Paul has just instructed the believers in Philippi to work out their salvation. And then he assures them he doesn't expect them to do so by their own effort. Rather they are to work out that which God is working in.

I've talked with hundreds of people about their ministry potential. And almost always I begin the conversation with, "What do you really want to do?" The answer to that question at least points them into a direction for ministry. So let me ask you, What do you really want to do?

Perhaps you're able to answer that question without a pause; you may even feel that special call to an area of ministry. In that case, you've taken the first step in choosing your particular ministry.

We can be confident that while God may be more concerned about our relationship with Him, He also delights in calling us to minister for Him when the time is right. But when He does call, we need to beware that one of the great traps we must avoid is that of becoming event-oriented rather than strategy-oriented.

But if you're experiencing indecision in your call to Christian service, there could be a couple of explanations:

Uncommitted?

First of all, you may not have the basics of Christian living in order yet. I'm convinced the dynamic that Paul speaks about in Philippians 2:13 comes as a result of nourishing the fire of the Holy Spirit in our own spirits. And that nourishing is the result of a commitment to the basics we detailed earlier in this chapter: a consistent devotional life, the regular study of God's Word, a serious prayer life, a desire to share the gospel with others and the pursuit of holy living.

We must be committed to these basics, if we are serious about ministry. God cannot challenge us with a special calling if we're not even committed to the Christian's general calling.

Timing Off?

A second reason for indecision could be the timing. Maybe the time just is not right. For the moment, God may want you just to focus on the general commitments of the Christian life. So He is not yet implanting any burning desire to pursue a special ministry. A critical lesson to be learned here is that God is more concerned about your relationship with Him than your ministry for Him. In this case, wait—and keep working on the basics.

EVERY MINISTER A STRATEGIST

We can be confident that while God may be more concerned about our relationship with Him, He also delights in calling us to minister for Him when the time is right. But when He does call, we need to beware that one of the great traps we must avoid is that of becoming event-oriented rather than strategy-oriented.

Many times churches make this dreadful mistake. They tend to repeat events such as the Sunday evening service, yearly revival, vacation Bible school and more, without asking strategic questions needed to evaluate those events. They get caught up in an array of repeated events without asking, Why are we doing this?

Strategists will ask certain questions about their ministries such as: (1) Who is my target for ministry? (2) Where are they located? (3) What are their felt needs? (4) How do I establish contact? (5) How can that contact lead to a sharing of the whole gospel? (6) If they respond to the gospel, how can they be enfolded into a healthy Christian community? Obviously, some ministries will demand different questions and considerations.

Unfortunately, lay people often believe all the strategy questions are to be asked by the vocational clergy. But unless clergy and laity alike outgrow that type of thinking, our churches will never see the unleashing of the God-given potential that exists in the Body of Christ. Now let's take a closer look at the questions every ministry strategist should ask.

Who's My Target for Ministry?

A crucial question that needs to be answered in the earliest stages of planning your ministry is, Who do you really get excited about and feel a burden for? Is it children, teenagers, young marrieds, singles, senior adults, businessmen and women? Whom do you relate to best? You will usually focus on those you feel most adequate with, but keep in mind there may be times when God will lead you to work with people other than those you are most comfortable with in order to teach you something new about depending upon Him.

Where Are They?

Very few lay people ever think to ask the question, "Where is my target group for ministry?" But this second strategy question is vital. It may help if we think about the Great Commission as it is stated in Acts 1:8: "But you will receive power when the Holy Spirit comes on you; and you will be my witnesses in Jerusalem, and in all Judea and Samaria, and to the ends of the earth."

So, four spheres—from local to distant—indicated in this verse: Jerusalem, Judea, Samaria and the ends of the earth. In which of these four spheres is your primary target group? Of course, we ought to be ready to minister to people in any of these spheres when the opportunity arises. But in planning a ministry, knowing where our target group is is key.

Into which sphere are you being called?

Sphere One: Jerusalem: For our purposes, let's call Jerusalem the local church. Sphere one is not an exotic place. The ministries such as Sunday School, visitation and choir are commonplace. But they are extremely important ministries. If you talk to 10 young people headed for the mission field today, my guess is the majority of them came to know Christ and made decisions to be missionaries in Sunday School, summer camp or vacation Bible school.

I dream of the day when the majority of lay people in our church will have had a cross-cultural mission experience. We are generally wise to spend more money on experience and less on things. Affluent Christians need to be challenged to buy less stuff and invest in going on short-term mission teams.

Sphere one is a strategic place to pour your life into ministry. We need faithful lay ministers who will live out their ministry callings to infants, children, teens and adults who are part of the church family.

A good example of this is in the life of D.L. Moody. Most Christians know that God used Moody in a magnificent way during the 1800s. Moody's impact isn't difficult to measure, for dozens of books have been written about his life and ministry.

But how many people recognize the name of Edward

Kimball? Kimball was Moody's Sunday School teacher when the future evangelistic giant was a teenager. Prior to attending Kimball's class at the Mt. Vernon Congregational Church in Boston, Moody attended a Unitarian church. Kimball wrote that Moody was not exactly a spiritual giant when he first showed up in class:

"I can truly say . . . that I have seen few persons whose minds were spiritually darker than was his when he came into my Sunday School class, and I think the committee of the Mt. Vernon Church seldom met an applicant for membership who seemed more unlikely ever to become a Christian of clear and decided views of gospel truth, still less to fill any sphere of public or extended usefulness."[1]

Fortunately Edward Kimball was not just going through the motions of teaching Sunday School. He studied to be an effective teacher, he prayed for his students and he went after them in order to introduce them to Christ.

On April 21, 1855 Kimball called on Moody while Moody was working in his uncle's shoe store. Right there in the store Kimball introduced this 18-year-old to a personal relationship with Jesus.

The answer to the who? question for Edward Kimball was teenage boys. The where? question was answered by ministering at the home base, in his Jerusalem if you will, as a faithful Sunday School teacher.

Sphere Two: Judea. Just beyond Jerusalem lies Judea, and just beyond the ministries that we have to our families and in our churches is the opportunity for friendship evangelism.

This sphere of ministry zeroes in on those who may not have taken the initiative to visit our churches, but are both geographically and relationally close by. We relate to these people in our everyday ebb and flow of life: our neighbors, work associates, business friends, fellow students and so on.

Sphere Three: Samaria. Once a Jew left Judea and entered Samaria, he was definitely aware he was in foreign territory. In our scheme of spheres, Samaria represents those who are geographically close, i.e. in the same city or area, but relationally they are distant. This sphere includes people in jails, internationals, those who live in senior citizen housing, abused children who are clients of the social service systems and more. In other words, these people live in our area, but we have no typical contact points.

Sphere Four: The Ends of the Earth. This sphere includes people who are neither relationally nor geographically close. While most of us won't become missionaries in the general sense of the word, we can benefit greatly by occasionally ministering in a cross-cultural situation.

I dream of the day when the majority of lay people in our church will have had a cross-cultural mission experience. We are generally wise to spend more money on experience and less on things. Affluent Christians need to be challenged to buy less stuff and invest in going on short-term mission teams.

These four spheres deal with the where? questions. When we've dealt with the who? and the where? we've just begun to strategize.

What Are the Felt Needs and Interests?

In sphere one, our family or our church, the greatest need is a sense of belonging. Recently I bumped into a man I hadn't seen for over 20 years. The moment I saw him I felt warm fuzzies. While I was in college, he and his wife had made Mary and me feel welcome in their young marrieds Sunday School class.

So when I saw him, I immediately thought again of his beautiful home. It wasn't a lavish home, but it was warm and friendly. Over the years, the Foxhavens have majored on making new people in their church feel welcome. Very few churches have a sufficient number of people committed to making new people feel welcome.

In sphere two, the needs are as diverse as are the people. The challenge here is to design diverse ministries, keeping in mind the felt needs.

For example, if you have a friend who is the mother of a preschooler, you both could get involved in a ministry like Mothers of Preschoolers (MOPS). If you know some sports enthusiasts, you might follow the example of some churches that sponsor "Sports Day" ministries. During the day, various sports events are held; then in the evening a spaghetti dinner is served and sports awards are handed out. As part of the program, a local sports figure shares his or her testimony. Another suggestion for a ministry in this sphere is to show a James Dobson video series.

The possibilities of creative ministry in this sphere are limitless. Why then aren't we seeing more of it? I suspect it's because we've left this strategy question up to the vocational leaders, and, quite frankly, we pastors aren't trained to think about ministries outside the church walls. Lay ministers must lead the way in this area.

In sphere three, we are dealing with people who are geographically close, but relationally they are distant—the abused children, jail inmates, foreign students and so on. The most consistent need in this sphere is one-on-one friendships. A friendship with a foreign student, for example, is normally something highly prized by someone who is lonely and confused by a new culture.

You are the key—you and millions of average lay people just like you! When you discover, develop and display your God-given potential for ministry, then we will see massive penetration in this society of the good news of Jesus Christ. We will see needs being met. And we will see changed lives everywhere.

How Do I Establish Contact?

As you think about basic questions like who?, where? and what are the felt needs? you will naturally wonder, "How do I establish contact?"

In spheres one and two, you already have contact. But in sphere three, making contact is a major challenge. The more you think through the types of people in sphere three, the more you realize there is almost always a power person connected with these groups.

For example, in the jail, the power person is the sheriff or program director; in an apartment complex, it's the complex manager; with international students, it's the foreign student advisor. Many times we have no choice but to work through those in power positions, but even if we can go around them, it's seldom wise to do so.

Recently this fact has become a painful reality for us. One of our ministry teams was told they can't return to the jail. A new program director took over at the jail; our leader clashed with the new director, and we were booted out. Even though the new program director is a believer, it's her responsibility to be in charge, and we had to respect her decision.

Most of the power people need assistance; if you work with them, they will welcome your participation.

SOME DO'S FOR AN EFFECTIVE MINISTRY

- Do your ministry as a result of your relationship with the Lord rather than to try to earn His favor.
- Do pray for and seek like-minded people to get involved with you; lone-ranger ministers often become casualties.
- Do specialize; learn the art of "this one thing I do," rather than "these 40 things I dabble at."
- Do discern your area of spiritual giftedness and work in areas of your strengths; it's very difficult to stay motivated working in your areas of weakness.
- Do learn to say no to things that are good but will sidetrack you from the best.
- Do commit yourself to being a lifetime student. In general, you pursue the basic spiritual disciplines and, in particular, you read, study and become a resource person in your special area of ministry.
- Do try to work out your ministry as a recognized part of your local church's ministry and remain accountable to the church's leadership.
- Do look for inner motivation; ask God what He wants you to do.
- Do realize that all ministries have highs and lows. When our Lord calls you to a ministry He doesn't promise you a rose garden.

- Do be faithful in the nitty-gritty work, even when there is little or no recognition.
- Do realize that the people who work with you, as well as those you are ministering to, may disappoint you from time to time.

SOME DON'TS FOR AN EFFECTIVE MINISTRY

- Don't fall into the trap of loving your ministry more than your Lord.
- Don't lay guilt trips on others for not getting involved in your ministry. Allow God to work in people and, until He does, assume the timing is not right.
- Don't let failures stop you; unless God makes it very clear He has shut the door, keep on trying.
- Don't neglect signs of burn-out; don't allow yourself to continue out of guilt motivation or out of a desire to please someone other than the Lord.
- Don't be afraid to quit when you have peace from the Lord that it's time to do so.
- Don't fall into the trap of "our ministry is more special than other ministries." It's a trap that tends to create first- and second-class citizens in the Church, and in Christ's Body there are no second-class citizens.

YOUR SPECIAL AREA OF MINISTRY

If the Church is to reach this generation for Christ, then

you, the average lay person, must find your special area of ministry. In the meantime, don't worry about those whom God has called into full-time vocational ministry. They have schools and lots of churches and organizations in which to serve. But in the end that relatively small group of professionals is not the key to evangelizing this generation.

You are the key—you and millions of average lay people just like you! When you discover, develop and display your God-given potential for ministry, then we will see massive penetration in this society of the good news of Jesus Christ. We will see needs being met. And we will see changed lives everywhere.

EXPLORING YOUR POTENTIAL

1. How would you rate yourself on a scale of 1 to 10 (10 being high) on the basics for Christian living as listed in the beginning of this chapter?

2. What are some of the questions every good strategist will use in determining the type of ministry to pursue?

3. What are the different spheres of ministry listed in this chapter? List the various ministry possibilities in each sphere, using the ones already suggested plus your own ideas.

4. Establishing contact with your target group is no doubt a major challenge. This chapter suggested several possible contacts. As you look at each sphere of ministry, can you think of others?

Note
1. "Edward Kimball Quotes Mr. Moody's Admission to the Church," *New York Witness,* April 1876 (Eleventh Week).

CHAPTER 10

Overcoming the Obstacles

Are there days when you feel like you just shouldn't have gotten out of bed? Chapter 4 of Nehemiah reveals that's the kind of day he had. Everywhere he turned there were problems. But then we might expect that when we read in verse 6: "So we rebuilt the wall till all of it reached *half* its heights, for the people worked with all their heart" (emphasis mine). The rebuilding project had hit the infamous midwall crisis point!

Now that I'm in my late 40s, I have some appreciation for that midlife crisis stuff. I'm convinced we can live the first half of life on sheer energy and ignorance. The pressing question in midlife becomes, Now that most of the energy is gone, and we know a few things, how do we keep on keeping on?

That question was raised by author and pastor Chuck Swindoll as he spoke at a pastor's conference some time ago. He lamented that as he traveled across the country, he found so few men his age still on the cutting edge. He was in his early 50s at the time.

Swindoll went on to tell of a black man, who was like an adopted uncle to him. He told how one day this uncle said to him, "Charlie, one thing you'll learn about life when you grow up is, it's so daily."

Life does have a way of taking the edge off things. It just keeps coming at us, ready or not. Once the edge is gone and we know too much, it seems more difficult to be excited and optimistic about anything.

The midway point of anything is a vulnerable time. It was no less true of Nehemiah, and it will be no less true with you in your particular ministry.

Nehemiah challenged the people of Jerusalem to rebuild the wall, and they hit the wall with so much enthusiasm that in a short time they had it half-built. But then we read: "Meanwhile, the people in Judah said, 'The strength of the laborers is giving out, and there is so much rubble that we cannot rebuild the wall'" (4:10).

What happened?

Nehemiah has two huge problems at this point in his rebuilding project: opposition from without and discouragement from within. These are both common problems in any project.

OPPOSITION FROM WITHOUT

The people of Judah found themselves working guardedly, each with one eye on the task and one eye looking over the shoulder, watching for the inevitable attack. Clearly, the relentless pressure was taking a toll on their morale: "When Sanballat heard that we were rebuilding the wall, he became angry and was greatly incensed. He ridiculed the Jews . . . . Also our enemies said, 'Before they know it or see us, we will be right there among them and will kill them and put an end to the work.' Then the Jews who

---

I'm sure life has a way of dumping as much rubble on your turf as it does on mine. What will it do for you? Are you committed to God-gazing or rubble-gazing? Maybe it's time for you to stop wanting *to grow closer to your Lord and to start* deciding *to do so, by having a quality daily devotional time with Him. After all, realizing your full potential for ministry depends on it!*

---

lived near them came and told us ten times over, 'Wherever you turn, they will attack us'" (4:1,11-12).

Opposition from Authority

If you become involved in a ministry, if you are willing to take a risk for God's sake, you can expect outside pressure. Pressure from without has been a constant reality for the people of God. Just as Israel had enemies from the beginning, so has the Church today. American Christians who travel behind the Iron Curtain inevitably come back with a feel for the incredible pressure their brothers and sisters must endure there.

It may be surprising to some that the twentieth century has produced more Christian martyrs than any time in history. When we think of enormous pressure on the Church, we tend to think of Christians being fed to the lions in Rome. Indeed, the Church did suffer brutal periods of persecution in the first, second and third centuries. But far more have died for their faith in more recent days.

Communism in Russia, China, Indochina and now Ethiopia has resulted in countless hundreds of thousands of martyrs. Then we must add to these the oppression of ruthless dictators in Third World nations and the fanatical Muslim states.

We Americans have a difficult time imagining what state-sponsored opposition is like. I'll never forget Eunis, a young Christian man from Tunisia whom I met in London. We were both staying at a guesthouse of the mission organization called Operation Mobilization.

During the dinner hour, Eunis said that he worked for British Airways and had used his flight privileges to come to London, not to see the sights, but for Christian fellowship. He explained that few Christians lived in his hometown of Tunis and they were under constant pressure from without. They were regularly cursed and harassed, as well as discriminated against in the job market and other social areas.

I continue to pray for Eunis and the millions of other believers who live with this ever-present pressure. I confess it's difficult for me to imagine the strain under which they live.

Opposition from Family

In the United States outside pressure is likely to come from sources much more subtle than a hostile government. A source of outside pressure that knows no political boundaries is that which is sometimes generated by our own families. "If anyone comes to me and does not hate his father and mother, his wife and children, his brothers and sisters—yes, even his own life—he cannot be my disciple" (Luke 14:26).

Some of the cults love to exploit this particular teaching. But it is safe to say that of all the outside pressures that can stand between an individual and his or her commitment to God, between you and your ministry, pressure from the family is among the hardest to handle. That pressure can be immense, especially if your family is not in tune with your commitment to Christ and your burden.

Opposition from the World

Outside pressure will always come from the world. The apostle Paul warns us about the relentless pressure in Romans 12:2: "Don't let the world around you squeeze you into its own mold, but let God re-make you so that your whole attitude of mind is changed. Thus you will prove in practice that the will of God is good, acceptable to him and perfect" (*Phillips*).

The relentless outside pressure for us is the temptation to conform to the value system of the world around us. A young lawyer—also a young Christian—and I were having our weekly Bible study. Before we parted I asked him how I could pray for him during the coming week. The first thing that came to his mind was to pray that he might be a genuine Christian lawyer, that he wouldn't get involved in immoral and unethical means to accomplish desired ends. I know nothing about being a lawyer, but I can imagine the outside pressure is great. The pressure of the world is great for anyone deeply committed to a Christlike life.

Throughout the rebuilding of the wall, Nehemiah was under pressure from without. And from the moment we seriously commit ourselves to Christ and His Work, we too are under this same kind of pressure. But as difficult as that adversity may be, pressure from without was not

Nehemiah's greatest problem in rebuilding the wall. Rather, it was something from within that caused his greatest delay.

DISCOURAGEMENT FROM WITHIN

"Meanwhile, the people in Judah said, 'The strength of the laborers is giving out, and there is so much rubble that we cannot rebuild the wall'" (Neh. 4:10).

Opposition from without for Nehemiah, our lawyer friend, for Eunis from Tunis or for you or me is no laughing matter. But it's not as deadly as discouragement from within.

In Nehemiah's case, the discouragement from within was brought about because there was just "so much rubble." The people of Judah became convinced they could not continue their work on the wall because the strength of the laborers was giving out.

Turning Our Gaze from God to Rubble

It was at the midpoint that the workers somehow lost sight of the reality that God was still God. They lost their motivation for their work. Instead of seeing God, they saw only rubble. And what happened to them happens to us, perhaps several times in the course of our lives.

The fact that the people of Judah were discouraged over too much rubble is especially interesting because there is no more rubble in chapter four than there was in chapter two! Jerusalem is not a rubble dumping ground for Arab dump trucks!

Yet in chapter two everyone was gung ho to begin.

They looked at the rubble and said, "We can do it!" Why were they so enthusiastic in chapter two? Because their leader had told them about the gracious hand of God on the project. He, like a good spiritual leader, had directed their focus toward God and, with their gaze upon their Lord, the amount of work didn't matter.

However, during those first three or four weeks it took to rebuild half the wall, a profound shift took place. It didn't happen all at once. A subtle shift, but it happened. Their focus shifted from God to the rubble. They started out as God-gazers but they became rubble-gazers. Day in and day out on the project, amid the rubble and constant pressure from without, their gaze shifted and they became discouraged.

Discouragement from within is not unique to Nehemiah's time. It is ever-present today in the work and ministries of God's twentieth-century people.

Becoming discouraged from within can result from many causes. Perhaps our finances run out, or our co-workers move away. Maybe personalities can't work together, or perhaps illness and fatigue take some of our helpers. Rubble comes in a variety of shapes and sizes. Whatever the cause, rubble is rubble, no matter how you cut it. And it's darned discouraging, for compounded rubble can become paralyzing to the work at hand.

Directing Our Gaze Back to the Lord

In Nehemiah 4:10, the people of Jerusalem were tired and discouraged; they had become rubble-gazers. Notice how Nehemiah handled the people when they were convinced they didn't have the strength to continue working on the wall.

"After I looked things over, I stood up and said to the

nobles, the officials and the rest of the people, 'Don't be afraid of them. Remember the Lord, who is great and awesome, and fight for your brothers, your sons and your daughters, your wives and your homes'" (v. 14).

Directing their gaze back to God was not only the right move to make, it alone would help them succeed. And at the end of chapter four, we read the results:

"So we continued the work with half the men holding spears, from the first light of dawn till the stars came out. At that time I also said to the people, 'Have every man and his helper stay inside Jerusalem at night, so they can serve us as guards by night and workmen by day.' Neither I, nor my brothers nor my men nor the guards with me took off our clothes; each had his weapon, even when he went for water" (4:21-23).

Unbelievable! These are the same people who, earlier in the chapter, were too tired to continue. Now they have the energy to stay on the wall from the first light of dawn till the stars come out. Why is that? The only explanation is that they have directed their focus from the rubble to their Lord.

Rubble-Gazing Plagues All of Us

My son and I were driving down a Denver street a few years ago when I pointed out a tall building and asked him, "Did you know your dad took a battery of vocational aptitude tests in that building awhile back?"

Totally surprised, he asked, "Why?"

"Because," I explained, "I wanted to know what kind of career I should pursue when I quit the pastorate."

I went on to tell him about the most extended and difficult rubble-gazing period of my life. I had family problems and ministry problems and I came very close to bailing out. I had thoughts not only of bailing out of the pastorate, but also out of my marriage. I wanted to bail out of being a

---

Satan will not watch God's work being done without trying to sabotage it from time to time. But God's people can take heart that God has already overcome the world. He has already conquered the enemy. We have already won the battle. And, if God ordains our ministry to carry on, it will carry on.

---

father. I fantasized about riding freight trains and living the life of a railway bum. As a young boy, I grew up in a rail-road town, and I learned a lot about life from the hobos who came to my father's restaurant. I was finding myself envious of their "no responsibility" lives.

What I remember most about that time of tremendous discouragement is that I was tired. I was tired when I woke up in the morning, tired after lunch and tired throughout the afternoon. I was eating right and I contin-ued to exercise regularly, but I was always tired. I remem-ber many times just stretching out on the floor of my office and staring at the ceiling.

I must admit, I have felt many times just like the peo-ple of Judah in Nehemiah 4:10. I have often felt like screaming, "There is just too much rubble. I can't keep on keeping on."

Fortunately, each time I have become a rubble-gazer, I have gotten back on track and have been able to refocus on my faithful heavenly Father who never takes His eyes off me.

Six years ago when I was barely hanging in there, I

took several days and went to a beautiful retreat grounds called Glen Eyrie in nearby Colorado Springs. I took my Bible and a copy of Chuck Colson's *Life Sentence*. God enabled me once again to shift my gaze from the rubble to Himself.

INTIMACY WITH CHRIST IS A CHOICE

If you're like I am, you find it difficult to spend time with the Lord in a devotional way every day. The ongoing pressures make it hard to keep my mind on having a quality relationship with Him.

Perhaps we should take a lesson from the Old Testament hero David. David *used* the pressures and circumstances of the day to have quality devotional times with the Lord. Over and over again in the Psalms, David is alone with God while under tremendous pressure. Maybe that's one of the reasons he is described as a man after God's own heart. Times of turmoil and stress often cause me to spend less time with the Lord.

Some time ago, I was at a pastor's conference where J. Oswald Sanders, who was 82 at the time, challenged several hundred of us to pursue intimacy with Christ. He shared a thought with us that I'll never forget.

He said, "Many of you want to be intimate with Christ, but you can look at your lack of commitment to a daily devotional time, and it's clear you have not chosen to be intimate with Christ." He taught us the difference between wanting to and choosing to, a difference worth pondering.

My guess is that you're in the same boat as I am. I'm sure life has a way of dumping as much rubble on your turf as it does on mine. What will it be for you? Are you committed to God-gazing or rubble-gazing? Maybe it's time for you to stop *wanting* to grow closer to your Lord and to start *deciding* to do so, by having a quality daily devotional time with Him. After all, realizing your full potential for ministry depends on it!

Perhaps the first step to overcoming opposition from without and discouragement from within is to realize it's going to be there sooner or later:

First, opposition from without is from the enemy. Satan will not watch God's work being done without trying to sabotage it from time to time. But God's people can take heart that God has already overcome the world. He has already conquered the enemy. We have already won the battle. And, if God ordains our ministry to carry on, it *will* carry on.

Second, you can expect discouragement from within from time to time. We do tire; we do move about the country more freely today than ever before; we will lose workers. And yes, we do have attitude problems. We are swayed and very often allow the rubble to come into focus.

But what cured the people of Judah can also be our medicine. We need to stop crying, fussing and worrying about the rubble and get on with the task. We need to have our vision refocused on or heavenly Father. And then He will supply all we need to finish what we have begun in His name.

EXPLORING YOUR POTENTIAL

1. Can you think of projects you began where you ran into snags at midpoint? What were some of the contributing factors?

2. What factors do you see as being opposition from without on just about any ministry you could choose to pursue?

3. What do you see as being potential discouragement from within?

4. How are Christians encouraged to be God-gazers instead of rubble-gazers? What is some of the rubble surrounding your situation? How can you direct your gaze back to the Lord?

5. Do you have a regular devotional time? If not, why not? If yes, what are the strengths and weaknesses of that time?

CHAPTER 11

Staying on Course

When I was discharged from the army, I knew times were going to be difficult. I wanted to go to college. Mary, however, was carrying our second child, and we did not want her working outside our home while the children were young.

So I decided to work a couple of jobs while attending school. It was difficult to see how I could possibly carry on any kind of ministry beyond the responsibilities of two jobs, school and my family. Yet, I really wanted to continue to be involved in some sort of ministry.

No matter how I looked at my schedule, the only time I had to conduct any ministry would be during my lunch hour. So I prayed specifically that God would give me a ministry for Him over my lunch hour.

In those days I lunched in two different locations. Some days, I spent time on the campus of Long Beach

City College and, on other days, I was selling shoes in downtown Long Beach. God honored my commitment by giving me a ministry in both places.

At the college I met some young Christians who had never had personal discipleship. We agreed to meet over the lunch hour to share memory verses and check with one another on our devotional times. I ended up discipling a young man by the name of Don for about three years.

A while back Don came through Denver and looked me up. We drove into the mountains to pray together. Along the way, he told me he had just returned from Turkey. He and his girlfriend had spent a very dangerous summer there. They had slept in fields and on the streets. They had both been put in jail for passing out Christian literature.

When Don had finished telling me about his summer, he began to recall our lunch hours in Long Beach. That was when Don's commitment to Christ had changed from that of a nominal follower to a dedicated disciple. His time in Turkey testified to his new dedication to Jesus.

My lunch hours downtown were different from those on the college campus. The shoe store I worked in was only a few blocks away from the Long Beach Serviceman's Center. The director of the center, Tommy Adkins, welcomed me there to witness to sailors. Whenever I was downtown, I would take my sack lunch to the Center, sit at a table with some sailors and share the gospel with them.

A few years after moving to Denver, I received an encouraging letter from Jerry, one of the sailors I had lunched with. Jerry told me that, although he had a hard time tracking me down, he persisted, because he wanted to say thanks for introducing him to Jesus one noon hour at the Serviceman's Center. During his time in college, Jerry had led the InterVarsity group on campus. He assured me he was still totally committed to Jesus. I'm convinced God allowed me to receive Jerry's letter just to assure me those lunch hours in Long Beach so many years ago were a great investment in his ministry.

Even though my schedule had been extremely tight, God allowed me to have an effective ministry in both discipleship and evangelism. As I look back on those hectic and busy times, I'm confident that effective ministry to others would have been impossible without a keen sense of priorities.

An endless stream of messages, tasks and events will try to lure us from what God has called us to do. As unique as God's children are, so will be the unique experiences that will aim to distract us from the business at hand. Only if we have set our priorities and realize the significance of what we are doing for God's greater glory, can we keep on keeping on. We can then stay on course.

IMPORTANCE OF SETTING PRIORITIES

I was very fortunate as a young convert to be born into a Christian community that made a big deal over setting priorities. As a new Christian, I was constantly being asked the following questions:

1. Are you keeping up in your devotional life and prayer time?

2. Are you spending quality time with your wife
   and children?
3. Are you studying and memorizing Scripture?
4. Are you sharing your faith with non-
   Christians?
5. Are you helping younger Christians grow in
   their faith?

The list reflects the kinds of things I was being held accountable for from the very beginning of my Christian walk.

Whatever strength there is in my Christian life today flows from the building of priorities into my life. Before becoming a Christian, I was basically self-centered. I wanted to get ahead, be happy, be appreciated and be my own boss. After becoming a Christian, I began to understand life as a mission rather than an accident, a mission with eternal significance.

Over the years I've learned that *significance* and *priorities* go together. When I was discharged from the military, I felt it was significant that I continue to have a ministry beyond my family. Hadn't Jesus' last command been to make disciples *everywhere?* I didn't feel I could put that command on the shelf for four or five years while I worked my way through college. So I had to be really disciplined about my priorities.

An endless stream of messages, tasks and events will try to lure us from what God has called us to do. As unique as God's children are, so will be the unique experiences that will aim to distract us from the business at hand. Only if we have set our priorities and realize the significance of what we are doing for God's greater glory, can we keep on keeping on. We can then stay on course.

SIGNIFICANCE OF GOD'S CALL

In the early '70s, the Westwood Housing Project on the west side of Denver was in turmoil. Young snipers fired at cars from rooftops. Gang fights were common, and crime was rampant. In response to this volatile situation, some churches in the area banned together and hired a street pastor to work with the Westwood kids. Through Westwood Ministries, I met Bud and Nellie Adams.

The Adamses live in Westwood and, during those turbulent days, they felt led to open their home to people who needed a place to live. For the first six years they worked with men, taking as many as 10 at a time into their home. Since their group home is not state-funded they have to raise their own support. Over the years, Bud has retained a full-time job to help pay the bills.

After six years, the Adamses switched their ministry to women, women who have been for the most part involved in prostitution, alcohol and drugs.

In the over 10 years Bud and Nellie have opened their home and hearts for this ministry, many things could have distracted them from their work. It has been a tough road with rarely enough finances to do what needs to be done. Bud and Nellie have been ripped off and mistreated. They live with constant heartache, as they personally see up close the human ruins. Yet they keep on keeping on. They continue to stay on course. Why?

Nellie will tell you: "We know we're called to this work, not because it's easy, but because God called us to it. It's not because our friends and relatives approve, but that God gives us the daily strength to do it. He has given the desire and ability to work with these people just where they are, at their level. It's fun to see the changes God does in lives. Most accept Christ and go on for schooling and jobs. In fact, when these people leave our home 90 percent of them are able to be independent. Success is up to God; our responsibility is just to be obedient."

Obviously Bud and Nellie keep on keeping on because they believe they are doing a great project for God.

RECOGNITION OF OPPORTUNITIES EVERYWHERE

One of the saddest commentaries on fortress-type thinking is that all the great ministries are those of the professional pastors. Churches recognize overseas projects, a traveling youth music ministry and so on, yet most of the potentially great projects for God remain unseen.

This truth came home to me in a fresh way a few months ago while I was in Boston. I was scheduled to preach at the historic Tremont Temple Baptist Church. I felt privileged to preach from the pulpit of G. Campbell Morgan in a church where Dwight L. Moody and Billy Graham have also ministered.

But on my return to Denver, my thoughts were not centered on the historical significance of this church. Instead I was preoccupied with a story that Tremont's pastor, Charles Hendricks, related. We were having breakfast with our wives at the Tremont Hotel, next door to the temple. Charles said that during the '40s, when the church was at its zenith in attendance, Ho Chi Minh was a busboy at the very restaurant we were enjoying that morning. I was stunned.

Imagine, the leader of the communist revolution in Indochina was once a busboy in this very room! And right next door to 2,000 Christians who regularly packed Tre-

mont Temple for worship services every Sunday morning.
Yet we have no reason to believe that Ho Chi Minh was
ever ministered to by a believer. The legacy of his hatred
for God and for the Western World is now a painful part of
world history.

Suppose, just suppose, someone at Tremont or somewhere else in Boston for that matter, like the famous Park
Street Church, which is only one-half block away, had been
convinced that God had called them to minister the love of
Jesus to foreigners in our land. Suppose they would have
been used to reach that seemingly insignificant little Asian
busboy. The course of history could have been altered.

On that plane trip from Boston to Denver, I couldn't
help but think of the difference between the story of Ho
Chi Minh in Boston and a man in Denver we'll call David.

David came to the U.S. from a country closed to the
gospel. While he was here he was befriended by some
who believe God has called them to carry on a great ministry for Him, a ministry called Friendship International.
They are also convinced that one of the most crucial ministries an individual or church can have is to minister the
love of Christ to foreigners.

The Friendship International team will tell you that
Scriptures often express God's concern for the foreigner
who lives among His people. They also know that many of
tomorrow's world leaders are in America today. They may
be busboys or waiters or they may be students on our college campuses, but one day back in their own countries,
they will often have enormous influence.

So these friends of David ministered the love of Jesus
to him. They also ministered to him from God's Word. As a
result, David invited Christ into his life and presented himself for believer's baptism. When David returned to his
own country, the Friendship International team didn't stop

ministering to him; they continued to pray for and kept in touch with him through letters.

Then one day one of the team members with face aglow handed me a letter from David, telling us that all members of his family had indicated their willingness to receive Christ into their lives. The heartfelt "alleluia" in his letter reflected the joy David was experiencing. At the same time, he realized that his family, as new Christians, still had much to learn, and he pledged to do his best in helping them to understand more fully these new beliefs they had embraced.

Because David knew his new task would be difficult, he requested prayer that he would have the strength and wisdom to adequately ground his family in the gospel of Christ. He also asked us to write him letters with stories that would continue to instruct him in the Christian faith, even as he, in turn, sought to guide his family into a deeper relationship with God.

It's important that a ministry be started because someone has the desire to start it, not because he or she has been made to feel guilty if the ministry is not begun. The impetus for ministry needs to be the positive call of God.

Since then David has sent us pictures of his beautiful family. To look at them and know they have passed from death to life in a country closed to the gospel makes me want to shout Nehemiah 6:3, "So I sent messengers to them with this reply: 'I am carrying on a great project and cannot go down. Why should the work stop while I leave it and go down to you?'" Notice that Nehemiah refused to be sidetracked by God's enemies because he was convinced he was carrying on a great project.

Great projects are everywhere. Working with an abused child, a senior citizen or a foreign student is a great project. Edward Kimball, Moody's Sunday School teacher, saw his class of boys as a great project.

But all kinds of things come along to sidetrack us from our ministries. Temptations to get involved in some sort of sin, even other good things that would detract us from the best. Endless voices beckon us to leave the work on the wall. But Nehemiah wouldn't leave, and neither will we, if we're really convinced our ministry is a great project for God.

QUESTION OF MOTIVATING PEOPLE

As I travel across the country doing "Unleashing the Church" conferences, certain questions always come up. One I can always count on is, What do you do in your church to motivate people to keep on doing difficult ministries?

Pastors tell me the biggest dilemma they face in their churches is the lack of motivation. And I share their frustration. Honestly, even in our church are many I have no idea how to motivate. From what I can tell, they just plow through the motions year after year without any sense of the exhilaration Nehemiah felt when he replied to the enemies of God, "I am doing a great project."

On the other hand, an unusually high percentage of our people are able to identify with Nehemiah's grand statement. So the question remains, How do you motivate people?

Motivation Is Positive

First and foremost, motivation needs to be positive. The key to motivating people is to create a climate where everyone feels free to respond to God's calling in their lives. For example, when someone feels led of the Lord to lead the church into a ministry to stepfamilies, that desire is recognized at Bear Valley just as someone's call to become an overseas missionary is recognized.

It's important that a ministry be started because someone has the desire to start it, not because he or she has been made to feel guilty if the ministry is not begun. The impetus for ministry needs to be the positive call of God.

Motivation Is Sense of Purpose

One of our former co-pastors, Roger Thompson, wrote in *Leadership* magazine: "A sense of duty isn't enough for long-haul motivation; a sense of purpose is."[1]

That's the motivation behind the incredible statement by Nehemiah. Many attempts were made to lure Nehemiah away from finishing the task to which God had called him. And each time, Nehemiah refused to be tempted, for he was doing a great project for God.

A sense of purpose is what motivates Susan Walker. Susan is a wife, mother and full-time admissions director for a Colorado Christian college. She is an incredibly busy person, handling a wide range of demands on her time and energy.

Yet Susan continues to direct our Life Unlimited ministry for unwed mothers. During a recent phone conversation, I hinted that she may be too busy to continue in the ministry. I tried to assure her it was OK for her to step down. Even if the ministry did not continue to operate, that would be better than her getting burned out.

Susan knows her limits and she assured me she wanted to continue. If you were to ask Susan why she is motivated to go on, she would tell you, "My personal interest stems from the fact that I have two beautiful adopted children. God has given me a burden to minister to the unwed mom. Our ministry exists to do more than address the abortion issue, and is available to an unwed mom for more than her pregnancy period. The demands of the ministry are not easy or convenient, but I'm confident this is what God has for me to do."

For years Allegra Donaldson worked in a state home for delinquent boys. Many of her kids eventually were "graduated" to the state pen, located a hundred miles away. Allegra not only stayed in touch with her kids through the mail, but on several occasions drove, regardless of the weather, to visit them. The state didn't pay her extra, nor did they expect her to stay in touch with the boys once they left her facility. But she believed that God had given her this ministry with those boys, and she was willing to go the extra mile.

The Adamses, Susan Walker and Allegra Donaldson are all compelled by their sense of purpose to stay on course and do the work God has called them to do. And that places their work high on their list of priorities.

Perhaps the single most important motivating factor they all have is that they believe they are pursing great projects for God. Their projects may not be impacting great numbers of people, but they are significant projects nonetheless. And because God has called these folks, they are motivated to keep on keeping on.

EXPLORING YOUR POTENTIAL

1. Many times our busy schedules do not allow for much in the line of ministries outside sphere 1, our own Jerusalems. Can you see little blocks of time in your life right now that could be used in ministry for God?

2. Setting priorities is key to not only unleashing our God-given potential for ministry, but also to living a sound and productive Christian life. How did you answer the five questions early in this chapter under the heading "Importance of Setting Priorities?"

3. What are some of the diversions that hinder you from accomplishing (1) personal goals, (2) work goals, (3) potential ministry goals? How best should you handle these diversions?

4. How motivated are you to set about unleashing your God-given potential for ministry? If you are involved in a ministry already, what do you need to do to keep on keeping on? If you are just considering a ministry what do you need to get you going?

Note
1. Roger Thompson, *Leadership*, vol. 1, no. 4 (Fall 1985), p. 85.

CHAPTER 12

God Works When We Pray

To see the usually upbeat Andy Cannon so discouraged was painful for me. We had worked together in the Coffee House ministry for seven years. In *Unleashing the Church,* I told the incredible story of how God led Andy and his family to Denver to lead our church into a ministry to street people. The ministry had gotten off to a great start. But now seven years later, Andy was wondering if he should even try to continue.

In 1977, God had placed a special burden for the street people of Denver on the hearts of five couples. Four of those couples were in our church. They had committed $600 per month to the yet unborn street ministry. The other couple, Andy and Linda Cannon, were working initially with street people in Memphis, Tennessee. But then the Cannons felt the Lord leading them to Denver to continue their work here.

The $600 per month that had been committed was a good start, but not nearly enough to run an effective ministry. We needed a group home, a couple of vehicles and some kind of business to run if we were going to provide jobs as part of the ministry. We also had to support Andy and his family. Nevertheless, we all agreed that God had begun putting the pieces together, and the Cannons should move to Denver as quickly as possible.

The Cannons began packing, and we all prayed. I'll never forget a Saturday morning prayer meeting that took place while Andy and his family were en route to Denver. I had anticipated that we would spend much of our time asking God for additional financial support. That had been the earnest request of dozens of prayer meetings in those days, and I was sure it would be so again that Saturday morning.

However, before we began to pray, one of our men handed me a check for $50,000! He had just closed a real estate deal and the seller had agreed to contribute $50,000 to our street ministry. The tone of our prayer meeting changed dramatically. Instead of spending most of our time asking for God's provision, we spent the time just praising Him.

In the early days of the street ministry, every step was bathed in prayer and God rewarded our faith. We opened a group home and started a business. Numerous commitments to Christ were made, and we as a church were making a difference in the lives of numerous street people.

Then after several years we lost the group home. The building we had rented for almost nothing was torn down to build a medical center. Once we no longer had a place for street people to stay, we also lost our business. Interest and excitement for the ministry faded. The problems we encountered on the street—homosexuality, addiction, despair—seemed to grow greater as our resources and commitment to this ministry diminished.

Of course, the people caught in the middle of all this were Andy and Linda. They were very discouraged and often felt like quitting. Working with street people had always been hard, and now the original fire and enthusiasm they had experienced when they first came to Colorado was gone.

The real battle Nehemiah fought and won was in his prayer life . . . . And it is true for you and for me.

Through the years Andy and I made it a practice to keep in touch and have lunch together. I had always looked forward to those times, but recently they weren't much fun. Andy usually had plenty of problems to share, but overall he had been upbeat and positive about his ministry. These days, however, he was consistently down. Everything with the ministry had turned sour. Only one other couple, Matthew and Mary James, remained alongside Andy and Linda in their ministry.

REALIZING THE POWER OF PRAYER

In January of 1985 Andy and Matthew committed themselves to a regular time of prayer. They decided to meet for two hours each Friday and ask God for several specific items, including:

1. A new facility for the Coffee House within the next four months. It needed to be much

bigger, but the rent had to remain the same.

2. Two new people a month, for the next 10 months, to get involved in the ministry. These would have to be people who attended either the Sunday worship services or the weeknight meeting at the Coffee House. They would not only need to be regular attenders, but also be committed to ministering to street people.

3. Two street people per month, for the next 10 months, to make serious commitments to Christ and to make themselves available for discipleship training.

4. By October, 10 months away, 40 people to be attending Sunday worship at the Coffee House. Forty would double their current number.

5. They and their wives to have their desires for ministry rekindled.

Little did the two men envision the incredible way God was going to answer their prayers.

It all began one evening when Andy and Linda invited Bill and Nancy White over to their home for coffee. The two couples didn't know each other well, but they hit it off immediately. The Whites had just returned from a short mission trip overseas with the YWAM (Youth with a Mission) organization. This ministry with YWAM just happened to be ministering to street people in Hong Kong. They shared with the Cannons how this experience had revolutionized their lives.

Andy and Linda's interest perked. They sensed that God had worked in the Whites's lives in an unusual way and, in the process, He had given them a genuine burden for street people. The Whites were the first of a steady stream of people to make solid commitments to attend the street ministry activities and to work with the people. By October, 10 months after they had begun to pray specifically for the Coffee House, Andy and Matthew could count 11 couples and several more singles who had become part of the ministry team.

When they had asked God for two people per month, it seemed impossible. Twenty solidly committed on the team by October sounded like a fantasy. In all the years he had worked with street people, Andy had never seen that many solid, stable middle-class people get involved with this ministry.

And when we consider the type of person Andy works with on the street, it's easy to see why getting people involved is so difficult. Nothing is glamorous about a street ministry today. In the '60s, young revolutionaries were in the streets, but that's no longer the case. Instead, we now find mental outpatients, displaced American Indians with chronic alcohol problems, runaway teens, addicts, a large number of physically handicapped people, prostitutes and dropouts.

Many are the forsaken, undesirable and often obnoxious people who can't get or hold jobs and are unwanted by society. They are unstable, confused, angry, and they want immediate relief from their enormous sense of pain. Of all the subcultures, they are the most difficult to relate to and disciple for the cause of Christ.

So it's little wonder Andy had never had many stable people volunteer to work with him. But then Andy will tell you that he had never persistently and specifically prayed for them either! It soon became apparent that God was not discouraged by the difficulty of recruiting people for this ministry. It also became apparent that the evening the Lord put the Cannons and the Whites together was just the beginning.

During each of those 10 months, at least two street people made commitments to Christ and availed themselves to be discipled. On the twenty-eighth day of February, both Andy and Matthew were aware that so far that month just one woman had sincerely committed her life to Christ. That evening the second serious convert made his decision to follow Jesus. God was faithfully answering their requests for two sincere decisions for Christ each month. Between the months of January and October 1985, at least two persons made genuine decisions each month, and occasionally God opened the floodgates. In one week during the summer of '85, Andy counted over 40 people who had made commitments to follow Christ.

Not only did God faithfully supply both the workers and the converts, He also supplied the new facility. That March, the Jesus on Main Street Coffee House (JOMS) moved into a new building that was five times bigger, while the monthly rent was only $50 more.

The new facility was a carpet warehouse less than a block from the old coffeehouse. Since it was around the corner and appeared to be part of a carpet store, Andy had never even noticed it.

The new facility had several advantages over the old one. It had a game room and a coffee area that could seat 100 people for Sunday services. Plus, it had a second level that could be remodeled to expand the worship area to accommodate 150.

Once the street ministry began to operate out of its new facility, the attendance at the Sunday worship service began to grow. By October, attendance had grown to about 80 people on the average Sunday. That was just twice the number Andy and Matthew had asked God to supply.

The final area of prayer that they consistently laid before the Lord was that He would rekindle their vision of the street ministry as well as the enthusiasm of their wives. God honored that prayer just as He did all the others.

Today, several months later, the ministry on the street continues to expand. My nephew Tom Tillapaugh and his wife Yvonne have moved to Denver to begin The Denver Street School. The school had three graduates at its first commencement. The beautiful graduation service was complete with diplomas, gowns, caps and class rings. A school for street people is not an easy operation to run. But Tom and Yvonne have the kind of commitment to Christ that allows them to live outside their comfort zones and run a difficult ministry.

Besides the street school, the worship service has developed into a full-blown church. That congregation is a wonderful blend of middle-class folk and street people, couples and singles, whites and minorities.

One of the key ingredients in unleashing our God-given potential is: First things first, realize the power of prayer.

When I consider the events that occurred in this ministry since January 1985, I am overwhelmed. God has raised up a church in the inner city. We didn't plan it that way. We didn't go to urban ministries workshops and try to analyze the situation and then proceed to start a church. Instead, two men faithfully prayed and, as a result, we are all witnesses to what God can do through the power of prayer.

PUTTING PRAYER FIRST

In the first chapter of Nehemiah, when the word came about the destruction of Jerusalem's walls, Nehemiah responded by going to his knees in prayer: "When I heard these things, I sat down and wept. For some days I mourned and fasted and prayed before the God of heaven" (v. 4).

Actually, the rest of chapter 1 is an example of Nehemiah's prayer life for the next four months. In verse 1 we read it's December and in chapter 2, verse 1 we're told it's April, and in between all Nehemiah did was pray.

We need to take a serious look at this leader's prayer life, because later when he went to Jerusalem, he faced one crisis after another. For example, remember in chapter 4, we read: "Meanwhile, the people in Judah said, 'The strength of the laborers is giving out, and there is so much rubble that we cannot rebuild the wall'" (v. 10).

The people were ready to quit! But Nehemiah was not! Instead he says, "Remember the Lord, who is great and awesome" (4:14). Those are the same words that began his prayer in chapter 1: "O Lord, God of heaven, the great and awesome God" (v. 5).

It's clear, Nehemiah settled his commitment to what God was calling him to in prayer. We could compare this to deciding whether or not to go jogging at 6 A.M. We had better decide that matter before we go to bed, not when the alarm goes off in the morning.

The apostle Paul warned Christians that we fight the real battle in prayer: "For our struggle is not against flesh and blood, but against the rulers, against the authorities, against the powers of this dark world and against the spiritual forces of evil in the heavenly realms" (Eph. 6:12).

The real battle Nehemiah fought and won was in his

prayer life. That's true for Andy and Matthew, and it is true for you and for me. One of the key ingredients in unleashing our God-given potential is: First things first, realize the power of prayer.

EXPLORING YOUR POTENTIAL

1. The power of prayer is incomparable. In this chapter we read how Andy and Matthew dared to ask God for several specific items. And God answered in incredible ways. When was the last time you asked God for something specific (1) in your life, (2) in your work, (3) in your ministry? How did He answer?

2. The number of people living in the streets is growing every day. Do you see potential for a street ministry like JOMS in your town? Would your church be willing to be involved? What steps could you take to investigate this possibility?

CHAPTER 13

How and Why God Makes Miracles

The headlines of the "Living" section heralded "The Miracle of 34th Street." The publication was the Sunday edition of our *Rocky Mountain News*. Sunday was also Christmas Day, 1983.

"The Miracle of 34th Street" is, of course, an appropriate Christmas title, but this miracle cited in our newspaper had nothing to do with the famous movie of the 1940s, *Miracle on 34th Street.*

HOW THE MIRACLE HAPPENED

Felt Need

The miracle of Christmas 1983 had to do with the revitalization of an area along the 34th Avenue in a run-down section of Denver. One of the major elements in that revitalization miracle was the opening of a medical clinic.

Committed Talent

This clinic was different from most of those set up in the poorer sections of big cities. Not a government-sponsored welfare program, this clinic was staffed by private doctors, nurses, dentists and counselors. But none of them was salaried; all were living off incomes from other jobs. These professionals donated a few hours to half a work week at the new clinic.

God wants to use you and me in a way that will make even His enemies take notice. They will see that it is God who motivates and enables us. And as a result of His blessing on our lives, we will, in turn, become a blessing to those in need.

For years, this ministry had been a dream of Dr. Bob Williams and his wife Jan. Bob, with Jan, who is a professional counselor, realized years ago they didn't necessarily have to leave the U.S.A. to use their professions as missionaries.

They had prayed now, for a couple of years, that the Lord would send Bob a partner to share his suburban practice. Whomever the Lord would send would have to be willing to live off half a normal physician's income.

God answered that prayer when He brought Duane and Marjann Claassen to our city. The Claassens had been involved in a Mississippi ministry, Voice of Calvary, for several years. Now the Lord had led them to Denver to help Bob and others open a medical clinic.

Flexible Ministry

The clinic has been open for several years now, and the miracle goes on. Scores of people have been ministered to on physical, emotional and spiritual levels. They have all received help on a pay-as-you-are-able basis.

HOW THE MIRACLE BEGAN

Jan Williams recently reflected on the beginnings of the ministry. She related that, during the early days of the clinic, they had time on their hands because the people of the neighborhood were skeptical of their motives and hesitant to come until Jan and her colleagues had proved themselves.

One day a young woman in her 20s ran into the clinic crying for them to hide her from her boyfriend, who was threatening to kill her. They quickly took her to a back room. While one of the counselors tried to calm her, the receptionist called the police.

Ann's story was that her boyfriend wanted her to start prostituting for him. When she refused he threatened to harm her and her children, so she ran. The police arrived just as the boyfriend was approaching the clinic. They were able to avert any harm and left with Ann and her children in their squad car.

Ann returned to the clinic several times for necessary medical attention. The Christian staff also shared with her about the Lord. They haven't seen Ann now for quite some time, but they are confident that they planted some seeds in her heart and continue to pray for her.

HOW THE MIRACLE CONTINUED

Medical Outreach

The medical needs of the low-income population are often quite different from those in the suburbs. An elderly woman once came into the clinic for some care. While she was there she asked if anyone could come to her home to see her husband who was an invalid.

When Dr. Williams arrived in their home he found the woman's husband in bed in a second-floor bedroom. The man had not been downstairs for over two years because his wife was not strong enough to help him, and they had no one else whom they could ask to help.

A social worker was contacted who later made arrangements for a male health aide to visit the home twice a week, move the man and help him become more mobile.

Spiritual Ministry

This kind of ministry is not only reaching those in need of medical attention, it is also touching the lives who are physically well, yet spiritually dead. Such is the example of Sharon.

Sharon had just completed her training to become a dental assistant; she was doing a required internship at a medical clinic. Another lady from our church, Evelyn, is a nurse who volunteers at the clinic on a regular basis.

Recently, Evelyn had just finished the Billy Graham

Life and Witness course. She was carrying a witnessing tool called "Steps to Peace with God" when both she and Sharon arrived in the clinic's lunchroom together. They had grown to be casual friends and Sharon felt comfortable sharing some of her problems with Evelyn.

Evelyn responded to Sharon by asking her if she knew the steps to reach God. Sharon was interested and subsequently committed her life to Christ. Sharon's life-style is more that of a street life-style than suburban middle-class. So Evelyn volunteered to take her to the services at the Jesus on Main Street Coffee House where Andy Cannon pastors.

WHY MIRACLES HAPPEN

Nehemiah 6:15 is a verse we've been waiting for: "So the wall was completed on the twenty-fifth of Elul, in fifty-two days."

But I think 6:16 is probably the best verse in the whole book: "When all our enemies heard about this and all the surrounding nations saw it, our enemies lost their self-confidence, because they realized that this work had been done with the help of our God."

So the World Might Know

Terrific! Jerusalem has once again become a center of God's strategy for fulfilling the Great Commission in the Old Testament. The enemies of God have been brought face-to-face with the reality of God via the work of His people. As far as Nehemiah's enemies were concerned there was not another way to explain the amazing feat of the wall being completely rebuilt in just 52 days.

When I saw the headlines of Christmas 1983, I couldn't help but think of Nehemiah 6:16. A secular newspaper realized that part of the miracle of 34th Street were people motivated by their Christian commitment to serve others.

My prayer for you, and I trust yours for me, is that today we will realize our full potential as ministers. Let's finish the task He has empowered us to do for God's greater glory!

When we observe what is going on in the Christian community today, how many of the success stories actually impress the unbelievers? I suspect that the unbelievers who see extensive poverty and need all around them are not impressed at all.

But when some committed professionals open a medical clinic in a needy part of the city the non-Christian world takes notice. Initially, they are probably skeptical. Many people, religious leaders and politicians alike, have used and abused the inner city for their own benefit. But when the world takes a close look and sees professionals willing to live on less to serve the poor, even they are impressed.

Of course, the objective of the Christian life is not to impress unbelievers. It's interesting though that when Paul listed the qualities of a Christian leader in his letter to Timothy he included, "He must also have a good reputation with outsiders" (1 Tim. 3:7).

So You and I Can Serve

God wants to use you and me in a way that will make even

His enemies take notice. They will see that it is God who motivates and enables us. And as a result of His blessing on our lives, we will, in turn, become a blessing to those in need.

In the Old Testament, God's people finished the wall to His glory. My prayer for you, and I trust yours for me, is that today we will realize our full potential as ministers. Let's finish the task He has empowered us to do for God's greater glory!

EXPLORING YOUR POTENTIAL

1. The couples involved in the miracle on 34th Street in Denver are using their professions as missionaries right in their own town. What is your profession? How could you use your profession in a ministry?

2. As you look inside your church, what are some of the professions represented there? Can you see potential for those professions to be used in local ministry? Name the various professions.

3. Nehemiah finished what he set out to do, to rebuild the wall at Jerusalem. And though we will begin and complete some tasks for the Lord, so much more needs to be done. What will it take for you to get involved and unleash your God-given potential for ministry?

Epilogue:
The Challenge

I wish you'd been with me these last few years to share firsthand the enthusiasm that the concept of unleashing the church has brought to people all over the United States and abroad. Speaking to church people about ministries beyond the church walls has been like bringing cool water to people in the desert.

I've received tremendous response from college students as I've spoken in their school chapels. When I've challenged them that we need a new generation with a new agenda for ministry in the local churches, a not unusual response is a standing ovation. That applause hasn't been for the speaker, but rather for a challenge this generation is hungry to hear, a challenge they know in their hearts is right.

A NEW MINISTRY AGENDA

We do need a new ministry agenda in local churches. Still generally true is that local churches provide service ministries to middle-class family units. By and large, if the middle-class doesn't require a ministry, we don't do it or even think about it. That's why we expect Sunday School, choir, youth ministry and so on. That's also why we don't expect the church to have jail ministries or ministries to abused children and unwed mothers.

But you and I can change all that. We can be part of a new generation with new expectations of our local churches. In fact, we need a generation that will *insist* our local churches be centers for dozens of new ministries, ministries that reach the middle-class families even more effectively, and ministries that go far beyond.

Individually, you will have to earn the right to have a hearing for your new agenda by demonstrating your convictions through your ministry commitment.

A RENEWED MINISTRY COMMITMENT

However, to make such demands and have such expectations, we must be prepared to see each other's God-given potential unleashed. And individually, you will have to earn the right to have a hearing for your new agenda by demonstrating your convictions through your ministry commitment.

This is a special hour for the American Church. We still

have a great deal of influence around the world. I say it's time we export a vision for the Church that's not based on superstar pastors, superbig facilities and up-front ministries. It's time we feature a brand of Christianity whose genius is masses of ordinary believers realizing their God-given potential as ministers for the Lord Jesus Christ.

Author's Note

An obvious omission in this book is the subject of spiritual gifts. Certainly Christians cannot see their potential realized without developing the spiritual gift(s) God has entrusted to them. But the topic of gifts is, in my opinion, too complex and controversial to be dealt with in the scope of this book. In fact, I recently heard a pastor I respect very much say that he would never try to help people discover their spiritual gifts because, he believes, persons are likely to change anyway as they grow older in the Lord. A great deal of confusion exists on the topic of spiritual gifts, and I feel no compulsion to add to it.

In our ministry, we encourage people to discover their gifts primarily through ministry. Some of the books we have found helpful in this regard are listed here in inverse order of their date of publication.

Wagner, C. Peter. *Your Spiritual Gifts Can Help Your Church Grow.* Ventura, CA: Regal Books, 1979.

Flynn, Leslie B. *Nineteen Gifts of the Spirit.* Downers Grove, IL: InterVarsity Press, 1973.

Yohn, Rick. *Discover Your Spiritual Gift and Use It.* Wheaton, IL: Tyndale House Publishers, 1974.

Bridge, Donald, and David Phypers. *Spiritual Gifts and the Church.* Downers Grove, IL: InterVarsity Press, 1973.

O'Connor, Elizabeth. *Eighth Day of Creation.* Waco, TX: Word Books, 1971.

Classified List of Parachurch Organizations

Alcohol Rehabilitation

Overcomers Outreach, Inc.
17027 E. Janison Drive
Whittier, CA 90603
(213) 697-2368

College Ministry

Campus Crusade for Christ Int'l
Arrowhead Springs
San Bernardino, CA 92414
(714) 886-5224

InterVarsity Christian Fellowship
233 Langdon Street
Madison, WI 53703
(608) 257-0263

The Navigators
P.O. Box 6000
Colorado Springs, CO 80934
(719) 598-1212

Children's Ministry

Child Evangelism Fellowship
P.O. Box 348
Warrenton, MO 63383
(314) 456-4321

Christian Counseling

American Association of Pastoral Counselors
9508A Lee Highway
Fairfax, VA 22031
(703) 385-6967

Christian Association of Psychological Studies (CAPS)
26705 Farmington Road
Farmington Hills, MI 48018

Community Development

Voice of Calvary Ministries
1655 St. Charles Street
Jackson, MS 39209
(601) 353-1635

World Vision USA-U.S. Ministries
919 W. Huntington Drive
Monrovia, CA 91016
(818) 357-7979

Cults

Christian Research Institute
P.O. Box 500
San Juan Capistrano, CA 92693

Shield of Faith
P.O. Box 19367
Denver, CO 80219

Spiritual Counterfeits Project
P.O. Box 4308
Berkeley, CA 94704
(415) 540-5767

Discipleship Ministries

Church Dynamics, Int.
Box 508
Vista, CA 92083
(619) 598-0909

Church Resource Ministries
Atlanta, GA
(404) 993-8446

Churches Alive
Box 3800
San Bernardino, CA 92413
(714) 886-5361

The Navigators
P.O. Box 6000
Colorado Springs, CO 80934
(719) 598-1212

Emergency Relief

World Vision U.S.A.-U.S. Ministries
919 W. Huntington Drive
Monrovia, CA 91016
(818) 357-7979

Food/Helps

Denver Leadership Foundation
COMPA—Food Ministry
1780 Bellaire Street—Suite 808
Denver, CO 80222
(303) 753-1370

Love, Inc. Church Services Networks
P.O. Box 1616
Holland, MI 49422
(616) 392-8277

World Vision USA—U.S. Ministries
919 W. Huntington Drive
Monrovia, CA 91016
(818) 357-7979

Handicapped

Christian League for the Handicapped
P.O. Box 98
Walworth, WI 53184
(414) 275-6131

Joni & Friends Handicap Ministries
P.O. Box 3333
Agoura Hills, CA 91301
(818) 707-5664

Health Care (For Needy)

Christian Community Health Fellowship (CCHF)
216 S. 45 Street
Philadelphia, PA 19104
(215) 387-0809

Christian Medical Society
P.O. Box 689
1616 Gateway Blvd.
Richardson, TX 75080
(214) 783-8384

Homosexuality

Exodus International
P.O. Box 2121
San Rafael, CA 94912
(415) 454-1017

Housing for Poor

Family Consultation Service
645 Grant St. SE
Atlanta, GA 30312
(404) 221-0015

Habitat for Humanity, Inc.
Habitat and Church Streets
Americus, GA 31709
(912) 924-6935

Hope Communities
P.O. Box 9620
Denver, CO 80209
(303) 292-4673

International Students

Association of Christian Ministries to Internationals
P.O. Box 1775
Colorado Springs, CO 80901
(719) 577-1054

International Students Incorporated
Star Ranch—P.O. Box C
Colorado Springs, CO 80901

Jewish Outreach

Jews for Jesus
60 Haight Street
San Francisco, CA 94102
(415) 864-2600

ABMJ/Chosen People Ministries
P.O. Box 2000
Orangeburg, NY 10962
(914) 359-8535

Legal-Conciliation

Christian Conciliation
Christian Legal Society
P.O. Box 1492
Merrifield, VA 22116
(703) 560-7314

Mental Illness Support

FRIENDS
10800 E. Jewell Avenue
Aurora, CO 80012
(303) 337-0333

Jobs

Genesis Jobs, Inc.
243 E. 19th Ave. #215
Denver, CO 80203
(303) 860-8904

World Vision USA—U.S. Ministries
919 W. Huntington Drive
Monrovia, CA 91016
(818) 357-7979

Mothers of PreSchoolers

Mothers of Pre-Schoolers (MOPS)
4175 Harlan St. Suite 105
Wheatridge, CO 80033
(303) 420-6100

Prison Ministry

Prison Fellowship
P.O. Box 17500
Washington, DC 20041
(703)759-4522

Pregnancy

Bethany Christian Services
901 Eastern Ave. NE
Grand Rapids, MI 49503
(616) 459-6273 or 800-BETHANY

Crisis Pregnancy Centers
Christian Action Council
701 W. Broad Street Suite 405
Falls Church, VA 22046
(703) 237-2100

Singles

Single Adult Ministries
4540 15th Ave. N.E.
Seattle, WA 98105
(206) 524-7300

Sports Outreach

World Sports
180 Harbor Drive
Key Biscayne, FL 33149
(305) 361-2058

Street Ministry

International Street Ministry Association
P.O. Box 27054
San Francisco, CA 94127
(415) 552-2300

Suicide/Crisis Prevention

Christian Helplines, Inc.
P.O. Box 10117
Tampa, FL 33679
(813) 251-4040

Contact Teleministries USA, Inc.
Pouch A
Harrisburg, PA 17105
(717) 232-3501

Unleashing Ministry

Newsletter and tapes,
2600 S. Sheridan
Denver, CO 80227
(303) 935-3597

Youth

Teen Challenge
444 Clinton Avenue
Brooklyn, NY 11238
(212) 789-1414

Young Life
P.O. Box 520
Colorado Springs, CO 80901
(719) 473-4262

Youth for Christ
Box 419
Wheaton, IL 60189
(312) 688-6600

Wilderness Ministry Training

Discovery Expeditions/Christian Encounter Ranch
P.O. Box 1022
Grass Valley, CA 95945
(916) 268-0877

Honey Rock Camp
Wheaton College
Wheaton, IL 60187
(312) 260-5124

Navigators Eagle Lake Camp
P.O. Box 6000
Colorado Springs, CO 80934
(719) 472-1260

Bibliography

Carr, John, John Hinkle, and David Moss III. *The Organization & Administration of Pastoral Counseling Centers*. Nashville, TN: Abingdon Press, n.d.

Colson, Chuck. *Life Sentence*. Old Tappan, NJ: Fleming H. Revell Co., 1981.

Halverson, Richard. *How I Changed My Thinking About the Church*. Grand Rapids: Zondervan Publishing House, 1972.

———. *The Timelessness of Jesus Christ*. Ventura, CA: Regal Books, 1982.

Henrichsen, Walter A. and William N. Garrison. *Layman, Look Up! God Has a Place for You*. Grand Rapids: Zondervan Publishing House, 1983.

Lewis, C.S. *Mere Christianity*. New York: MacMillan Publishing Co., 1964.

McKenna, David. *Megatruth*. San Bernardino, CA: Here's Life Publishers, 1987.

Steinbron, Melvin J. *Can the Pastor Do It Alone?* Ventura, CA: Regal Books, 1987.

Stevens, R. Paul. *Liberating the Laity*. Downers Grove, IL: InterVarsity Press, 1985.

Tillapaugh, Frank. *Unleashing the Church*. Ventura, CA: Regal Books, 1982.

Trueblood, Elton. *The Incendiary Fellowship*. New York: Harper and Row Publishers, inc., 1967.

Viscott, David. *Risking*. New York: Simon & Schuster, Inc.; Pocket Books, Inc., 1983.